By Loren K. Keim   Copyright © 2010

ISBN 978-0-578-04868-0

Address: 2299 Brodhead Rd, Suite J, Bethlehem, PA 18020
Phone: 484-893-3004
Fax: 610-866-6075
Email: gideonpublications@yahoo.com

Acknowledgements

The 25 years I've spent as a Real Estate Agent and Broker have been an exciting adventure. The people who have helped me in my career are too numerous to mention, but I do want to thank some of the people who have significantly contributed to this book (while hopefully not leaving anyone important out):

Theresa Keim, Tim Mahon, Ellie Barrett, Wayne Talaber, Joe Bartera, Deb Hartman, Keri Schlosser, Don Blose, Marc Lucarelli, Elmer Heiney, Christa Klein, Mike Miller, Michelle Miller, Holly Weiss, Cathy Mahon, Bob Wilfinger, George West, Elmer Heiney, John Stangl, Francisco Sainz de la Peña, Kathy Reither Ziegler, Bob Hartman, Tom Young, Jeff Sell, Balji Minhas, Becky Hite, Ruth Wuchter, Todd Siegfried, Tom LaDue, Niko Pitsilos, Karen Ackerman Pitsilos, Cindy Bartera, Neil Szanyi, William Bader, Chris Bracy, Joe Stumpf, Ralph Williams, Tom Cooke, David Zinczenko, Chris Bracy, Stephen Thode, Geraldo Vasconcellos, Kathleen Clayton, Mary Pat DeJarnette, Rick Petko, Curt Cameron, Mary Hudock, Rudy Amelio, Linda Becker, my children (Bridgett, Caitlin, Logan and Kourtney) and many others!

I also want to thank the person who assisted me with editing and compiling all this information: Betty Broadbent

Cover Art was done by Anthony Giest of Ghost House Studios

Primary Editor was Mary Linn Roby

Table of Contents

Chapter 0:
An Introduction to Life

It's a typical crazy Monday at my real estate office in Allentown, Pennsylvania. In the front conference room, a frantic mother, having recently lost her husband in a traffic accident, and unable to afford the mortgage on her own, needs me to help her figure out a way to keep her two children from losing the only home they have ever known.

In another room down the hall a man and woman both having recently lost their jobs, leaving them unable to afford the mortgage payments on a house which, in the current market, is worth less than what is owed on it, need advice on a short payoff with their lender.

However, I haven't been able to meet with either party yet because I'm on the phone with a third client whose family homestead is deeded in his mother's name. The nursing home, where she is currently living, has informed him that according to Medicaid, the house, which has been in the family for five generations, must be sold to pay part of the cost of her care since federal regulations will not allow the property to be retained by either her or the family.

In desperate need of help, and on hold with our Medicaid client, I head to Michelle Miller's office on the other side of the building, where I am greeted by whoops of laughter and other indications of a celebration initiated by the fact that the young couple with whom she is meeting have just received word that their bid on a unique stone farmhouse has been accepted by the seller.

"What's up?" Michelle asks, looking up at me.

"I guess you're too busy to help me right now," I say. "Is Mike around? I'm feeling a little overwhelmed."

But it seems that Mike is up at the house of Rick Petko, one of the stars of television's Orange County Chopper. Our phones have been deluged by callers who want to see Rick's home, but who are probably not qualified to buy it, making it necessary for Mike to attend each showing in order to weed out nosy fans.

To further complicate matters, Frank Langella beeps me on my cell with news that our favorite Academy Award nominated client, who is presently appearing on Broadway, and is considering a Pennsylvania farm as a weekend retreat, is not impressed by any of the properties that we had sent him. He needs, Frank tells me, seclusion, in a location that will be under an hour and a half commute from New York. As I mentioned, it's a Monday.

Life doesn't come with an instruction manual. We learn by watching and by doing. We test our limits, make mistakes, and hope we don't accidentally kill ourselves while doing it. And given all the idiotic things that I've done in my time, I'm constantly amazed that I'm still breathing and walking. Some of the mistakes have become learning experiences that I'll share with you in this book.

So who am I? Over the past two and a half decades, I've been a successful real estate broker in Pennsylvania, just north of Philadelphia. In the world of the real estate agent, we are in a position to observe people and situations at their best and at their worst. If we're careful, we can learn from the pain, resilience and triumph of others.

For good or bad, I've had the opportunity - or the misfortune - of quite often being in the right or wrong place at the right or wrong time. Many years ago, a good friend of mine wrote an online article called "Loren Keim, the Human Accident Magnet". It was an amusing piece that garnered a lot of attention which I eventually asked him to remove from the web because I was afraid that, funny as it was, it was affecting my business, particularly since the article was so popular that Googling my name produced it up front, with the result that, instead of potential clients reading about my accomplishments in the field of real estate, they would find themselves engrossed in accounts of my various misadventures.

The fact that I have experienced an unusual number of unique encounters really came home to me in September of 2005 at a relocation meeting I was attending in Las Vegas when a group of us, on our way from the Aladdin Resort, now known as the Planet Hollywood Resort, to Paris witnessed an accident in which a driver jumped the curb with his Buick and ran down fourteen pedestrians on the sidewalk, killing three. As a result, that evening, sitting around a dinner table with about a dozen other real estate brokers, managers and relocation directors, the conversation turned to stories about near-misses to which I contributed an account of the time when a drug dealer fired a gun at an agent of mine and me, missing us by a few inches.

Someone changed the conversation, trying to add a lighter tone with "What about funny stories or anecdotes?" at which someone brought up the fact that she had recently assisted one of the stars of the TV sitcom *Everybody Loves Raymond* with purchasing a second home. I, of course, then shared two quick stories of celebrities I had worked with over the past few years including an academy award nominated actor and a famous rock star.

"Wow!" a woman at the table exclaimed, referring to one of the names I had dropped. "He's been one of my favorite actors forever. I love his movies. The only famous person I've ever met was a mentor of mine, and that was before he became famous."

"That's wonderful." I replied. "I had a mentor a number of years ago. He's a brilliant person, a former realtor and entertainer. I'm told he is now a coach for some of the top minds in the country."

One constant in the universe is that when one "salesperson" tells a good story, all the other "salespeople" around a table need to one-up them. And after each great story, I'd add yet another of my own. The first three or four stories clearly impressed them, but after the sixth, they started looking skeptical. Clearly I was coming across as a very skilled liar, or someone who belonged in a mental institution for the criminally deranged. All my stories were true, of course, but most people live within a certain paradigm of their surroundings and have difficulty accepting people or situations that don't fit within their personal bubble of comfort, just as they can't believe that so many different experiences can be part of an individual person's life. But I assure you they can. I once told a colleague that I have the same experiences everyone else does. I simply have them more frequently.

For years, I've tried to guide my clients, friends and the realtors in my company in the direction I felt was best for their home sales, careers and life by relating some of these experiences, with the result that I have been urged to write a book about them, which is precisely what I have finally done.

What follows then are some of my best and worst experiences, as well as some of my thoughts on society and politics. I hope you will not only enjoy but learn from them. After all, the old line to the effect that those who do not study history are doomed to repeat it is true. I believe we can learn a lot about human nature, relationships, finances, economics, and overcoming pain by simply watching, listening and learning from those around us.

Stop living the "sound bite" life of those who watch only the headlines and form opinions without ever really understanding the underlying nature of a subject. To quote Ferris Bueller, "Life moves pretty fast. If you don't stop and look around once in a while, you could miss it." Cue the music.

The Eldorado and the police...

About twenty years ago, when I was just beginning in real estate, I had invited friends of mine who were thinking of investing in property to my house for dinner, along with my girlfriend, after which we drove in my car, a big Cadillac Eldorado, over to the office to go through the Multiple Listing System. By the time we were finished, it was quite late, and none of us were particularly pleased when, having piled back into my car, we discovered that it would not start. So I called one of the most important emergency services in the country. Yes, I called AAA.

Life Lesson: We should always listen to the advice of others and carefully consider the opinions of those who know more than we.

The tow truck driver, who was dispatched in response to my panicked call, looked over the car and announced that he *could* get the car started but it wouldn't make it very far. Even though he explained the problem, I was sufficiently mechanically challenged, not to understand it precisely. But the point is that, being young, macho and just plain stupid, I decided that since it was only a few miles to my house, where everyone had left their cars, I would make a run for it. And since the mechanic had told us that we had an electrical issue, I felt it would be better to drive with no headlights, and therefore we should stay off the major highway and just take the surface streets.

So, slightly after midnight on a Friday evening, I drove at a relatively high speed down Hamilton Street to Hanover Avenue in Allentown and took a short cut through a parking lot to try and save as much time as humanly possible, in the process of which I passed a police car going the opposite direction. I suppose it should have come as no surprise to me that the police cruiser spun around and, with sirens and lights flashing, proceeded to pursue me.

Making a quick turn around the corner, I pulled over leaving the car in park, naively assuming that I could simply explain to the officer why I was driving with no headlights and that he would certainly let me go the last mile to my home. As I went to open the big door of the Eldorado I noticed a police car pull up next to me in addition to the one that was now behind me, and another car approached from the other direction pulling up in front of my car, boxing me in.

Putting the car in park, and starting to get out, I turned to my companion, and over the noise of the loud engine said, "Keep your foot on the gas pedal, we're going to have to get out of here quickly". In the process of stepping out of the car, I somehow managed to trip over my own foot and land flat on the ground at one of the officer's feet.

To add a bit more context to this story, I should probably inform you, that having all but cut off my middle finger several weeks before by slamming it in the car door, the doctor at the Muhlenberg Hospital Center who had sewed me back together, had cast it with a metal bar on either side of my middle finger. As near as I can determine using hindsight, the police officers, seeing me take a dive with a metal object in my hand, assumed that I was armed.

Suddenly officers were diving behind their cars, drawing their guns as they did so. "Lie face down!" someone shouted. "And push that weapon away from you!"

I, of course, had no idea what they were talking about. After all, my only problem was that my headlights weren't functioning. So naturally, I stood up and said, "What are you talking about?"

And then, since they were all shouting at once, I got back in the car and shut the door, only to find myself caught up in a spotlight. Needless to say, when all of us were forced to get out of the car while the officers searched it, my friends and potential clients, not to mention my girlfriend, were far from pleased.

As it turned out, the police had been responding to the burglary alarm at a bank in the shopping center parking lot when they found themselves being passed by a large car with no headlights, with the result that they had pursued the car. Needless to say, they were extremely unhappy with this turn of events. Having bigger fish to fry, they eventually let me go.

The next day the five of us were at McDonald's on Union Boulevard in East Allentown with a group of probably fifteen other friends, busy recounting the story of what happened the night before. My friend Tom was in the process of making a few well chosen disparaging remarks about the incompetence of police officers in general, and one in particular, when he realized the rest of us were staring at him wide-eyed, and turning he saw the gentleman in question standing right behind him, arms folded across his chest and an unpleasant expression in his eyes.

I had never before seen someone actually faint.

Hidden in the Attic...

During the course of the last decade, most real estate companies conducted so-called caravans, by which I mean that all the realtors in any given office inspect all the new listings that have come on the market over the prior seven days, in order to acquaint them with the company's current inventory. Many companies still do this although, in my opinion, it's a wasted effort since the agents could be more usefully employed actually marketing the available homes.

Consequently, we stopped this practice a long time ago, replacing it with broker's open houses for unique properties.

In any event, several years before, one of our agents, Christa Klein, had brought in a listing of an all brick split level in the west end of Allentown, a beautiful house that we scheduled first on our caravan tour that coming Tuesday.

> *Life Lesson: If someone doesn't want you to visit... there might be a good reason!*

As always, our receptionist called the owners to verify the Tuesday morning appointment to view the home. When Tuesday came, we joined two dozen other realtors at the house. I rang the doorbell and received no response, which was odd because the owner had definitely said that she'd be home. After knocking loudly and again, received no response, I decided to use the lock box on the front door. I had just begun spinning the dials when the door flew open.

The woman answering the door, presumably the owner, looked dumbfounded at seeing such a large group of people assembled in her front yard. "What are you doing here?" she asked, whereupon Christa took the lead, explaining that we were caravanning new listings and we were going to take a quick walk through the house just to get a look at the general layout.

But, she protested, the house was dirty. Couldn't we come tomorrow instead? And when I explained that Tuesday was our day to do caravans, and went on to assure her that we would look past the grime, she protested that she had dishes in the sink. And when I told her that would not be a problem, she told us that she'd be right back and shut the door, only to reappear a few minutes later and lead us down to the basement, muttering something about giving her time to straighten up a little.

This was early in my career and most of our office was made up of women, so I was attempting to show off my vast knowledge, having just completed a construction course, and believing I actually knew something about it. As a consequence, I was busy explaining the type of electrical service in the house and the size of the beams when the owner reappeared and told us we could go through the rest of the home.

We stepped up into the family room and looked around, and then proceeded to the next level to look at the dining room and kitchen. There were a good many dishes in the sink in the kitchen, but certainly that didn't detract from the nice oak cabinets and solid surface countertops.

Finally, we proceeded to the upper level and looked last at the master bedroom, which had its own bathroom and a walk in closet in which there was a trap door that allows access to the storage area of an attic.

Since there was a chair positioned directly underneath the trap door, I suggested that we take a look at the attic insulation and at the same time find out how much room there was for storage. But when I raised the door, I was surprised to find myself face to face with a pair of men's bare legs, and looking up, saw that the gentleman in question was outfitted in nothing but boxer shorts.

"I'm working on the attic fan," he said in a singularly unconvincing way, hoping no doubt to put us off.

But realtors are a curious bunch, and in the end every single member of my office staff wanted to also climb up on the chair and look at the man in the attic. This took about fifteen minutes. When we returned to the kitchen, we found our hostess pacing back and forth, wringing her hands. Then, pulling herself together with an obvious effort, she explained that the man in the attic was there to help her pack.

We later learned that the owner had been transferred to Texas where he had already started working while his wife remained at home to oversee the sale of the house.   The sad part of the tale is that the husband called us two days later and told us he wanted the house removed from the market, because, he said, his wife was unhappy about the way we were "servicing" the property.

Needless to say, we failed to mention the man in the attic which she was apparently "servicing" very well.

My First Sale

Over the years, I've read a lot about the great American work ethic, but I have yet to see signs of it in the general population. Perhaps I'm being cynical, but I believe the reason "get rich quick" books, audio programs and workshops sell so well is that most people are looking for a way to get around the hard work and long hours that lead to individual success.

Life Lesson: Investigate each situation before taking action. Don't rush in without all information.

The field of real estate sales is a classic example of this. In most areas of the country, a person simply has to take a course or two and pass a state licensing exam. Then whammo, they become licensed to assist buyers and sellers with their most valuable assets: homes, land and businesses.

Each year, I interview a few dozen newly licensed agents who tell me that they're becoming realtors because the earning potential is virtually limitless, often adding that since my firm is well known they would be glad to help take advantage of all the buyers and sellers who are, clearly, desperately in need of their services. I can't begin to calculate the number of fresh new realtors who have come to me, nurturing the notion that, if they show a half dozen homes to a young couple, and write an offer, they can make ten thousand dollars. How tough could that be, they say?

It's true that the earning potential of a realtor can run into the millions. However, building a multimillion dollar career in real estate means working exceedingly hard, taking on the difficult tasks that most people would never dream of tackling.

Now, please don't misunderstand me. I make a great deal of money by teaching licensed realtors techniques to improve their ratios and dramatically increase their incomes. However, a newcomer must put a lot of effort and time into building their personal business in order to be successful and avoid becoming a statistic in the extremely high fall-out rate of licensed Realtors.

Most new realtors sit at their desk, or hang around the water cooler, while waiting for that big break to show up on their floor time. I know that I started my career with the same mistaken beliefs. For my first few months in real estate, I bought into the myth that I could simply wait in the office for the phone to ring. Actually, when my first client *did* appear, it was one of the worst things that could have happened to me.

He called me after seeing a "For Sale" sign on a property our office had listed on South Fifth Street in Allentown. Prepared to do everything right, I called the owner of the home and left a message saying that I'd be showing the house later that afternoon. We set up showings through an index card system. Each home had an index card with showing instructions, and we were to follow the showing instructions and then write our name and the time on the card so the listing agent would know who had been at the property. We simply had to let the owner know we were showing it, leave the showing time on their answering machine, and use the lockbox on the front door.

Just after one that afternoon, I drove to the home, a three story brick row home with a covered front porch, to find my new clients already there. I rang the bell and knocked on the door. No one answered, so I dialed the combination on the lockbox and called out as I opened the door, just in case the owner was home and hadn't heard us knocking.

Like most Pennsylvania row homes, this one was long and narrow. Just inside the front door, a long staircase led to the second floor, while to the right, a long living room – dining room combination stretched to a kitchen at the very back. After viewing the first floor, we heard a muffled noise as we proceeded up the long staircase. When my client asked about it, I explained that, although sometimes they might hear something from an adjoining home, I was certain that their privacy would be insured by the brick, lathe and plaster walls which separated this townhome from the next.

The couple did not seem particularly impressed by the size of the bedrooms on the second floor. They mentioned that their bedroom furniture wouldn't fit in the relatively small front bedroom of the second floor. Additionally, the noise persisted, and I was concerned that the couple would not purchase the home because the walls were obviously less thick than I had assumed.

However, when we reached the third floor, which my notes told me featured a large master bedroom suite, we found ourselves in a room with a mirrored ceiling and walls, in the center of which, on a king sized bed, the owners were absorbed in enjoying some mid-afternoon delight, an exercise made all the more striking by the fact that it was reflected above us and on every side.

I'm fairly certain my cheeks turned several shades brighter. I had, I admit, never thought of voyeurism as a sales gambit, but the fact was, that despite everyone's embarrassment, the buyers made an immediate bid.

Oddly enough, however, I never received a referral from the sellers.

Sometimes gratitude is too much to hope for.

Chapter 1:
Why Selling Homes is a Challenge!

Although home buyers are usually ecstatic when they find the perfect home in the perfect neighborhood, working with sellers can be a challenge, primarily because they often entertain the illusion that their home will sell for a higher price than is reasonable, given the current market conditions. Needless to say, we realtors love the fact that the seller often blames us when a buyer doesn't materialize as quickly as the seller's desire.

Home sellers have a difficult time accepting the fact that their price might be too high or today's buyers aren't purchasing the home because of the lime green shag carpeting that was installed in 1967. Instead, it must be the realtor's marketing efforts that are to blame for the lack of an offer. Over the years, I've been told by more than two dozen clients that I simply need to run a big display ad in the *New York Times* and buyers will appear at their doorstep. Unfortunately, it doesn't work that way, and for the cost of a display ad in the *New York Times*, I could probably *buy* the house.

One client actually suggested that we hire a celebrity or entertainer to put on a show at which we could sell raffle tickets, thus luring potential buyers by offering them the possibility of winning the property. When I suggested that no doubt Robin

Williams would drop everything and do a comedy routine for us, I don't think my attempt at humor was appreciated.

Many clients also believe they know more than their realtor. After all, they've lived in the home for many years and believe they know which features are most likely to attract the best buyers, and since they have the nicest home in the neighborhood (everybody does), it should sell easily.

Unfortunately, home sellers often talk their way out of sales when they get the opportunity to either control the advertising or marketing or actually meet and negotiate with the buyers, which is a polite way of stating that many home sellers do really dumb things when trying to sell their homes. There are definitely times when an impartial third party between the buyer and seller can certainly help bring the sale to a close.

Selling a home at a busy intersection...

Some of the unwise things that home owners say when they're trying to sell their home constantly amaze me. Sellers, being emotionally invested in their property, are often their own worst enemy, making statements that absolutely cost them a sale.

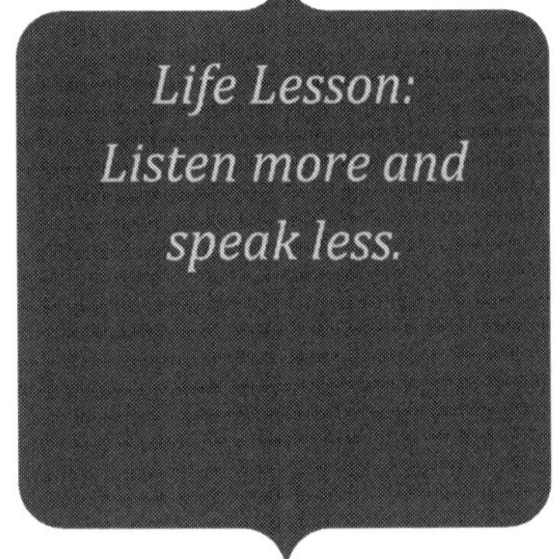

As an example, a few years ago, I had a young couple named Stacey and Dennis, looking at a property along a very busy road near Whitehall, Pennsylvania for the third time, a house that was located at least a hundred feet off the road, behind a line of trees, but was only one door off a major intersection. The layout reminded Stacey of her grandmother's home, and she also appreciated the convenience of being very close to a major shopping district.

Dennis loved the convenience of the home's proximity to his work, just five minutes away. Neither was bothered by the noise from the busy intersection, which apparently, was the primary complaint of potential buyers who had looked at the house previously.

As we were about to leave for the office to write up an offer, the seller pulled into the drive, and hurried out of his car towards us. "Wait a minute, wait a minute," he yelled, waving his arms. "Come back to the house. I want to show you something."

Given the circumstances, I could scarcely refuse, and in a few minutes we were standing in his living room.

"Do you hear that?" He demanded triumphantly, shutting the solid oak front door.

"Hear what?" I said.

"Nothing! That's exactly what I mean. You don't hear anything once that door is shut. There's no sound whatsoever. This house is so well built that you don't hear noise when the door is shut."

Assuring him that that was wonderful, I began to shepherd my buyers back outside.

"You don't understand!" he said, positioning himself between us and the door. It's really, really quiet in here. You can sleep without having to worry about being awakened by the noise."

"Uh, okay." I replied, displaying my command of witty repartee.   His emphasis on "the noise" was beginning to unnerve me.

"As a matter of fact," he continued, "there's a major accident every single week at the corner down there, and sometimes we don't even hear the sirens."

It was beginning to be perfectly clear to me that if I allowed him to continue in this vein, he was going to jinx the sale.

"Okay, that's fine. I'm sure the buyers appreciate that".

"You know, there are ambulances and police on this corner all the time because of the accidents," he confessed enthusiastically.

"And we don't even hear the sirens. That's how well built this house is."

"That's wonderful. Thanks for your time," I responded once again.

He put his hand out, frantic that we were trying again to leave. "No, no, no, you really don't understand," he said. "For example, my son's best friend was killed on our front lawn last year. He was pulling out of our driveway and got T-boned on the main road right out there." He pointed behind him toward the front door. "His car rolled over into our front lawn. We had ambulance, fire trucks, and police in our front lawn with lights going, and sirens flaring, and we didn't hear a thing. That's how incredibly well built this house is."

My buyers and I were flabbergasted. Looking back at Stacey, I saw that her mouth had formed a perfect "O", which was not surprising, given what she had just heard. On the way back to the office, her husband said, "Well, if we purchase the home, we'd have to buy a really big shop vac to suck the blood out of the front yard, won't we?"

It came as no surprise to me when they decided not to make an offer on the house which, eventually, sold for significantly less than the original asking price.

Sellers have to be really careful about intervening between their realtor and the potential buyer. Of course, no reliable realtors should fail to meet the state's requirement of full disclosure. However it is not necessary to introduce the possibility of offering a property which will give the buyer a front row seat to scenes of horror, featuring gore and dismemberment.

Watch out for flying cars...

I encountered a similar situation this year while taking clients through a property adjacent to a raised four lane divided highway, which ran about forty feet above the home's back yard. Standing out back on the rear patio of the property, it was hard to miss the loud sounds of tractor trailers screaming by at sixty-five miles per hour. It was so loud that, when we inspected the back yard, we had to yell to be heard but the most unfortunate thing was that the seller was present.

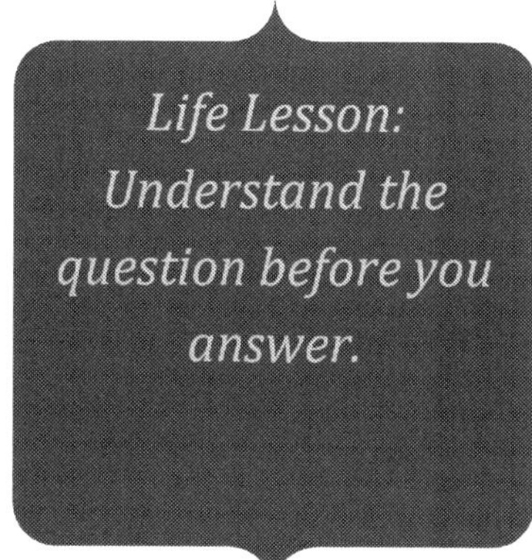

When the seller joined us on the patio, and asked what we thought of the property, my buyer told her that she loved the house, and thought the price was reasonable, but as she put it, pointing at the highway, "I don't know if I could live with this."

"You know," the seller said, obviously annoyed. "I keep hearing people complain about the highway, but I really don't see a problem with it. You know, we've lived here for over twenty years, and there's only been one occasion when a car has flipped over the guard rail and ended up against our house. And it's really not very likely that it will happen again. Either way, I'm sure no car will ever flip over and crash through the house."

A stunned silence followed this announcement. I was not surprised when this buyer changed her mind as well.

The Ceramic Dolls

Out of the thousands of clients I've assisted in selling a home over the years, I've only twice been asked by home owners *not* to show their home to people of some protected class or minority. In both cases, I carefully explained that we cannot exclude anyone from viewing, offering on, or purchasing their home because it would be discriminatory. Besides being illegal, it's wrong, and I won't do it.

Oddly enough, in both cases, the very first interested clients were people from that particular protected class group that the owners wanted to avoid. Sometimes life simply seems to work that way.

I've had several home owners ask me to refuse to show their rental properties to women with children, because they believe children will damage the property. Again, it is absolutely against the rules to discriminate and we don't practice discrimination in any form. Strangely enough, every time someone makes a request like that, the first people through the door always seem to have an inordinately high number of children.

Some of my client's requests make me recall Bill Cosby once saying *"God has a sense of humor."* This sense of humor rears its head in the most interesting circumstances in life. For example, a client named Ted once presented me with a unique request. He was looking to purchase a twin home in Whitehall or Catasauqua and requested that I prescreen any homes he and his wife viewed because he wanted to be absolutely certain that any houses he looked at did not have ceramic or porcelain dolls.

I had heard some strange requests in the past, but I had to ask, "Ceramic dolls? I don't understand."

"Everyone has some fear in life. Some people fear falling. Some people fear enclosed spaces and avoid elevators. Do you have any fears?" Ted asked me.

"Strong women." I replied.

> *Life Lesson: Always keep your promises. Part of a strong character is doing what you say you will do.*

"Excuse me?"

"Just kidding." I said. "I'm not a big fan of heights and I actively avoid roller coasters; especially the ones that go upside down."

"My wife has a fear, a very significant fear, of ceramic dolls. She knows that she's being unreasonable, of course, but she has recurrent nightmares about their coming to life. That's her fear and I'm respectful of it."

"Well, I guess that makes sense," I said. "After all, some people are afraid of clowns."

"All I'm asking is that you make sure that you preview any houses we're interested in seeing to make sure there's no ceramic or porcelain dolls there."

Of course, I said, "No problem, that won't be an issue." I tried to tell myself that I'd heard more unusual requests although, just at the moment, I couldn't think of any.

On the day that I was supposed to take Ted and his wife to view properties, I had planned to preview the houses in the morning, and then take Ted and his wife out in the evening to see the homes. Unfortunately, I was tied up, arguing with attorneys and other brokers over a pending transaction. The late afternoon was marked by heavy downpours and so I didn't make it to preview the homes.

To avoid being caught in a bad situation, I called each of the listing agents, and asked if they had noticed any ceramic dolls around the house. I was able to reach each agent that had an occupied property, but unfortunately, was unable to connect with the listing agent for the final property. Because that property, according to my notes, was vacant, I had no qualms about showing it.

That evening, we looked at the first three homes without incident, and they all showed fairly well. By the time we pulled up to the last listing, it was late in the evening and rapidly getting dark. Fumbling with the lockbox, I finally extracted the key and opened the front door.

Peering in, I discovered that it was far darker in the house than on the porch. Unfortunately, since the light switch was not right inside the front door, as it is in most homes, I had to cross the room, searching for it, Ted and his wife close behind me.

When we arrived at the far right hand wall, I clicked on the light switch, and to my surprise and horror, discovered that three of the four walls were lined with shelves and shelves of ceramic dolls. One of our agents, Joe Bartera, often says "You can't make this stuff up." Unfortunately, reality truly is stranger than fiction, and our story isn't quite over.

Against the far wall, presumably between the dining room and the kitchen, there was a large ceramic doll that was almost life size, perhaps four and a half to five feet tall, which, when I took a step back, incredulous at the sight, proceeded to topple forward, sending the wife screaming out the front door, never, sadly to return.

The Shotgun in the Foyer

People have varying concepts of what is "normal". In another case, I was trying to list a home for sale in a dense urban area where there had been a recent shooting. Sales were slow in the neighborhood and several nearby homes had been boarded up. Many row-homes in the area had been converted to multi-unit apartments and were deteriorating.

Jake, the home owner, was trying to convince me that his home was worth significantly more than what my analysis had shown, pointing out that his sister had recently sold a very similar home for a much higher price only a mile away in the same city.

My response was to simply explain that his sister's home was in a far different location. Although it was the same city, his sister's neighborhood commanded higher average prices than his, possibly because it didn't have lots of boarded up houses and reputation of being a violent crime area.

"I'm always hearing that crime is a problem here," the owner declared, clearly agitated. "This is not a bad neighborhood. There is no crime problem."

"Well," I explained, "perhaps the media *has* put too much emphasis on some crimes that have occurred here, but the news reports have impacted the public's perception of the area. Fewer buyers are willing to live in this particular area. Then, too, there are lots of homes for sale, and that tends to force the prices down."

"It's all a myth, Mr. Keim," he told me vehemently. "There are no problems in the neighborhood. I'm telling you there are none. Sure, people come up on my porch every so often, and sure they try to force my windows open, but that happens everywhere."

"Oh." I said, thinking that my wife would have moved out after the first attempt to force the windows open.

"Do you see the shotgun standing behind the sofa?"

"Uh, yes." I said. After all, I'm never at a loss for words.

"Whenever someone tries to mess with me or my property, I step out on the porch and point that shotgun at them. They all scatter. It works all the time. They don't stand around trying to fight or anything like that. They just run. That's the sign of a good neighborhood. Nobody's really looking for a fight."

Unfortunately for Jake, the home couldn't be sold for the amount he needed. In the end, he rented the home to tenants until the mortgage was paid down.

> *Life Lesson: People are partly products of their environment. We should attempt to understand and communicate from their point of reference instead of ours.*

Viewpoints like this aren't limited to real estate, of course. We're all a product of our environments. We are conditioned by our circumstances in life. For example, many of my clients, over the course of time, have expressed very strong opinions about solving the Middle East crisis. These are people who grew up in quiet neighborhoods with sidewalks and tree lined streets, where everyone waves to each other as they pass and all their kids play soccer on weekends which, no doubt, is the reason that, not being able to see beyond their own boundaries, so many of them believe that all we need to do to persuade all the radicals and terrorists of Afghanistan, Iran and Syria to stop terrorist attacks is to simply go there and show them we love them. I can't begin to tell you how often I've heard that if we could only be nice to people, they would be certain to be nice back, a dramatically alternate view to that of Jim Quinn, host of the *War Room* on XM Satellite Radio, who says, "There is such a thing as evil, and you cannot negotiate with it.[i]

When clients give me this lecture, my response is usually to ask them, "Let's say you were in a dark alley, being mugged at gunpoint because you had more money than the mugger and he felt that you owed him, or because he felt powerful threatening you and taking something from you. If you simply gave the mugger a big hug, would he turn and walk away?" This, unfortunately, leads me to lose potential clients and drive some people into short rages and rants about American imperialism, as if *that* started more than two thousand years of war in the Middle East.

There are people in this world who have been brought up to believe that it's okay to strap bombs to their children and send their children into marketplaces to kill others. There are people in this world that have been raised to accept as true that anyone that doesn't share their religious beliefs are infidels and must be driven from existence.

Certainly, this is not the belief of most Muslims. However, even though not everyone in Baltimore is a mugger or crack-head either, I wouldn't walk down a dark alley at two in the morning there. Our safest course, in my opinion, is to make a point of understanding the beliefs and perspectives of other people, instead of assuming that they are like our own.

Ghosts – How to Sell a Haunted House

The term "historic" is relative depending on your point of reference. Several years ago, a client, relocating from London, asked us to find her a newer home, and since she made a point of the fact that she didn't want something "old", we set up showings on homes that were built within the past three years only to find upon her arrival that, her point of reference being London, she was actually willing to consider anything built within the last fifty years.

Over the past few years, I've spent quite a bit of time in Saint Charles, Missouri. I absolutely love the Saint Louis metro area, but I find it funny how often the residents ramble on about how incredible it is to live in an area that is really *old* and *historic,* by which they mean anything that dates back to the days of Lewis and Clarke. These are people who would probably be shocked to learn that there are homes in Bethlehem, Pennsylvania, where I've spent most of my career, that predate Saint Charles by about 200 years.

Allentown and Bethlehem are very old cities when compared with most of the country, with some homes dating back to the 1600's, which helps to explain the number of ghost stories that are connected with various properties. In one instance, my team listed a historic bed and breakfast for sale, a gorgeous three-story Victorian style house which featured a beautiful turret and a wrap-around porch decorated with very intricate latticed woodwork. The home was located in a coal mining area, where most of the coal mines had closed.

But as far as the owners were concerned, the attractiveness of the property, which had been built at the turn of the century, was not the most important marketing ploy since they were convinced that the house was haunted, not simply by one apparition, but by three. They told me that their guests traveled from all corners of the country in hopes of catching a glimpse of these restless spirits, Pamela's favorite being the one that now and then marched through one of the second floor bedrooms, looking as human as life, except that it walked about eighteen inches above the floor. And although I never personally saw a ghost, goblin or ghoul, I did manage to sell the house for them in relatively short order.

Because of my success with this unique property, I received a call from the owner of another like it, a two hundred year old house located in Allentown. The owner specified that I arrive between seven and ten after seven in order to see the ghost which, he claimed, made an appearance every evening at precisely 7:17 pm.

Sure enough, seventeen minutes past seven, on the dot, there was a slam of a door on the second floor. The dog perked up his ears and stared at the staircase that stretched down to the kitchen and the hair on the back of my neck stood up as I heard the steps creaked as if someone was coming down them.

The dog appeared to follow the wrath's progress with his eyes as it moved through the kitchen and out onto the back porch. I actually heard the screen door slam, despite the fact that, to my certain knowledge, it never opened or closed. Once the apparition was gone, the dog once again rested his head on his master's lap.

The owner claimed that since this event happened each and every night, this was his ticket to a high price for his home since a haunted house would attract buyers from far and wide.

Whether the home was truly haunted or this was an elaborate hoax, I thought the idea was terrible. Who in their right mind would buy a home simply because they believed it to be haunted? The bed and breakfast had sold because of its many unique characteristics. However, if a buyer is planning to purchase a home, whether or not he or she believes in ghosts, he or she is probably not taking the chance on meeting one in the middle of the night, when there are plenty of other homes out there to purchase.

However, Brian's enthusiasm convinced me that perhaps some other avid ghost enthusiast would appear to purchase the home, and as a consequence, we advertised the property locally and in the tri-state area for months, but no one even came to view it. In fact, I received calls from competing agents who thought I was completely out of my gourd.

We contacted newspapers and expanded our marketing and our search for a buyer further and further. No one looked. The owner eventually grew tired and removed the home from the market.

The Ghost Next Door

A few years later, we had a nice couple interested in purchasing a beautiful bi-level style home in a suburban neighborhood in Salisbury Township. Sadly, a brutal murder, which had captured national attention, had recently taken place next door. A trio of high school aged boys had formed a group of skin heads and viciously murdered their parents and brother.

Shock ran through the community. This was a quiet, unassuming township where things like this simply didn't happen.

When they learned about this, our buyers withdrew their offer on the home next door. I, of course, attempted to convince them that the neighborhood was really quite safe and that this was a one-time occurrence that could not have been predicted, particularly since, not only had there never been any murders in that neighborhood, there were no street gangs and very little crime. In fact, most local residents slept with their doors unlocked. Furthermore, the three boys had been arrested and were likely to go to prison forever.

"I'm not concerned about someone committing a similar crime," the wife assured me in a matter-of-fact-way. "I'm worried about the ghosts."

"What ghosts?" I exclaimed.

"The ghosts of the murdered family members," she patiently explained.

"But it wasn't *this* house. It was the house next door."

"What if they float down the street to this house?" She asked me.

"What if they… *what*?" I said.

"I expect our deposit back," she said, and without another word, she turned and left me staring after her, speechless.

Out of Africa

One of the critical components of selling a house is staging the interior in order to appeal to the greatest number of prospective buyers. The great challenge of this is to find a way to assist home owners to understand that, as nice as their house may be, they are in competition with dozens, if not hundreds, of others that are very similar to theirs. Buyers make offers on those homes they feel are the best value, which are invariably the homes that give buyers a good feeling.

A house that's been freshly painted in a neutral color not only shows much better against competing properties, but is also more likely to set off the buyer's current belongings to best advantage which is why they have the widest appeal.

Despite this fact, home owners continually argue with me when I try to assist them in obtaining top dollar for their properties.

"I've put too much money in this home already," they say, "and the buyer will probably want to choose their own colors. I'm not investing another dime in this house." The interesting dynamic is that when that same person tries to sell a car, he probably washes it, waxes it, vacuums it and may even tune it up. A home that shows well will attract far more money than a shiny car, yet many owners won't put the effort into maximizing their sales price through staging.

To complicate matters further, over the years I've run across home owners who've made surprisingly poor decorating choices. Certainly, we still run across the occasional goldenrod or pea green appliances, carpeting that's been in place since 1962 and a wide variety of cheap paneling. These are always challenging, but I'm speaking of situations that are worse by far.

For example, about fifteen years ago we sold a home in Bethlehem, Pennsylvania, many of the rooms of which the owner had painted black, and not only just the walls but the ceilings as well, which was a problem, not only because dark colors make rooms look smaller, but are difficult to cover with other shades unless surfaces are completely primed.

Fortunately, I was able to find buyers who loved the location and size of the home, and were willing to repaint the entire home. Unfortunately, not realizing that the walls needed to be primed before being painted, they had to put four or five coats of white on the walls until the gray went away.

Several times in my career, I've been in homes with florescent colored rooms. Some owners have explained that a book or parenting program back in the 1970's had shown that children who read in rooms painted with fluorescent colors tend to retain more. I have no idea whether or not that is true, but it is very difficult to sell a home in this condition. Buyers will walk through the home, staring at the walls, and tell me "Wow, what were they thinking?" And when, later, I ask what they thought of the property, they often say that they had been too caught up in the color schemes to really look at it, or they'll do an impression of John Travolta in Saturday Night Fever, ending the conversation.

My favorite poor decorating choice was in Macungie, Pennsylvania where the owners had set up the home to reflect their view of Africa. The home was a bi-level style residence, which basically means it was a ranch home raised partly out of the ground to allow for living space in what would normally be considered the basement.

In this particular case, the owner attempted to install the flavor of the African plains into every room in the home. The living room featured green shag carpeting, which I believe was supposed to represent grass, although shag had gone out of style several decades earlier. The peaked ceiling consisted of bamboo shafts.

Bedroom doors were replaced with hanging beads, which tends to limit one's privacy, and sink handles were replaced by something that looked like tusks. Some walls had images of giraffes, gazelles, trees and similar scenes.

The home sold for far less than a typical bi-level in the same area because a buyer had to be found that was willing to renovate the house back to a state of normality. A buyer who has to work on a home will usually overestimate the cost of the renovations and then take off an additional percentage for the trouble and time they have to go through in order to actually perform those renovations. Every once in a while we get lucky and find the "perfect" buyer who falls in love with the unusual decorating, but in the case of the "home out of Africa", I believe there was only one family who appreciated the novelty of it, and unfortunately, they were the ones selling the home.

Chapter 2:
Human Nature... It's a Funny Thing

I have always been a student of human nature, and it has been my observations that people are not all programmed the same. For example, when an emergency or a disaster strikes, some people find the courage and strength to help those around them. In any disaster, there are stories of heroes bursting upon the scene, pulling children from fires and risking life and limb to save complete strangers. Many of these heroes appeared to have been regular people going about their daily lives until they were called upon to make extraordinary efforts.

At the same time, down the street, there are people who, as soon as that disaster strikes, hop into action by looting storefronts and the homes around them. What causes people to react so differently? Can it possibly be innate in their natures, inherited from their families, or is it possible it is bred into them by their upbringing, their surroundings and friends? It is the old question of nature or nurture.

In the real estate industry, we see people at their very best and their very worst, since often people buy homes during exciting times in their lives, at the time of their marriage, or the birth of their first child. Some buy real estate to punctuate a new promotion or their rising careers. These clients are anxious and excited and fall in love with the new home.

On the other hand, many people sell homes because of a divorce, a job loss, a forced relocation or a death in the family. Some experts have written that moving is the third most stressful time in a person's life after death and divorce. Unfortunately, in our line of work, we get to see the effects of divorce and death on those left behind. When selling a property, people are at an emotional peak, and often, are not thinking as rationally as they should. This can lead to some highly interesting situations.

I Hit Your Car

Tim Mahon, a managing broker with our firm, parked his car in a lot on his way to visit a client after being careful to lock it. On his return he noted that someone had hit the back passenger side causing significant damage to the bumper and tail light. He looked around to see if he could find the culprit but none was in sight.

On the front windshield was a folded note, tucked under the wiper blade, read:

*Life Lesson:
Beware - People are
not always honest
and trustworthy.*

To the owner of this car:

*I'm sorry, but I accidentally hit it. I feel badly about that.
There are many witnesses, so I'm writing you this note.
Everybody around me thinks I'm writing you my name and my
phone number. I'm not.*

The Second Hot Dog

A big sign across the front of a mini-mart near our office announced two hotdogs for ninety-nine cents. On his way back from an appointment, Tim stopped to take advantage of the deal but found only one hotdog on the grill.

"Do you have more dogs in the back?" he asked the store manager.

"No, sorry, we're fresh out."

"That's too bad. I've been on the road all day and I could probably eat four." He placed the last hotdog on a bun and brought it to the counter.

"That's ninety-four cents," the store manager announced.

"How much?"

"Ninety-four," he replied. "That's eighty-nine cents for the hotdog and five cents tax."

"But the giant sign in your window states two for ninety-nine."

"That's true, but you're only purchasing one."

"But you only *have* one. If you had two, I'd buy two."

"I don't, so you're buying one, so it's at full price."

Tim, having a strong opinion of right and wrong, proceeded to explain to the manager that this was not only unfair, but misleading and he should honor his advertising.

This mini-mart is the only place in the Lehigh Valley that Tim is now banned from entering.

Don't Inspect the Pool

Buyers and sellers have both been known to fib. For that matter, some realtors have been known to exaggerate the truth as well. Buyers may tell us their income is much higher than what they actually earn, which is always interesting since the lender generally requires paystubs or a verification of employment (VOE) which asks the boss how much the buyer makes. In probably a hundred of more cases in our company, we've worked with buyers who "forgot" they had a car loan, despite the fact that the mortgage officer specifically asks if they have any such loan, or simply didn't remember that they had a bankruptcy two years before. By the way, credit reports catch these situations.

Life Lesson: The world is not always nice or fair.

I try to remind all clients that they need to be completely open and honest so that we can work out their challenges before they find a home, negotiate and apply for a mortgage. Of course, I generally give this speech during the initial interview with a buyer, when they first come into the office and explain to me all of what they want in a home and how much they're willing to spend. Then we all have a good laugh, because there are no multi-million dollar mansions currently for sale under fifty thousand.

Home sellers might neglect to tell us that they are in foreclosure and the sheriff sale is only ten days away, or they might mislead us in the reasons for selling. My most frustrating situations are when a seller "forgets" that he has six feet of water in the basement every spring, or that he filled a leaking oil tank in the back yard with concrete. "Gee whiz, I completely forgot that we buried that toxic waste out back, Loren. Sorry, but it's an honest mistake!" Buyers are somewhat protected by seller disclosure laws and by home inspections, but that doesn't stop some people from trying to hide issues.

In Emmaus, Pennsylvania, shortly after the leaves had fallen from the trees and just before the first snow fall of the season, a seemingly sweet older couple put their home on the market. A young couple, represented by our firm, fell in love with the brick home and made an offer to purchase the property, which featured a large in-ground pool surrounded by a patio. The young buyers loved the location and the layout of the home and they were excited by the prospect of having a pool for the first time.

Their offer was contingent upon having a home inspection to verify there weren't any significant repair issues that would put stress on the buyer's budget after moving into the home. When the inspector arrived to go over the house, the home owner explained that the pool had been winterized and sealed with a cover to protect it for the winter. He assured the inspector and the young buyers that the pool functioned perfectly and could be opened easily in the spring. The owner even gave the buyer a disclosure in writing that the pool was operating properly and had, to his knowledge, no physical defects. The buyers were satisfied and settled on the home. After all, why would this nice older couple lie?

The following spring, the new owners uncovered the pool to find it completely empty of water and cracked across the bottom. They called me, distraught at this turn-of-events. When I called the former owner to ask if he had any idea how this could have happened, he once again assured me that he had never experienced any problem and was shocked and saddened to hear that the pool was damaged. Of course, he said, it had been a harsh winter and perhaps the pool cracked because something had shifted in the ground. He felt he had no responsibility since the pool had failed after he sold the home, which was true if the damage had occurred subsequent to the buyer's taking possession.

Our buyer selected a pool company at random from the yellow pages and asked someone to come give an estimate to repair the pool. The estimator looked around, scratched his head, and said "I've been here before." Opening his metal clipboard, he flipped back a few pages and discovered that he had given an estimate to the prior owner to repair the pool as recently as the summer before.

As a result, the former owner denied any liability or wrong-doing right up to the time of a mediation hearing, at which point he reluctantly gave up and paid the cost of the pool repair. Sometimes luck is on the right side. Had the new owners called any other pool company, they might never have discovered that the damage had been hidden by the prior owner.

The Angry Husband

One of the primary reasons that married couples divorce is over money. Husbands and wives are not necessarily always honest with their spending habits. In some cases, each may actively hide their spending from a spouse by hiding the receipts and the credit card bills. This can be easily accomplished in many marriages because one of the spouses often handles all the finances. Sometimes, a spouse may take out several credit cards and make the minimum payments on one card by paying it with another. If you play this game, you will eventually be caught.

A few years ago, Bob Wilfinger, a mortgage broker that works with our firm, attended a home settlement. The buyers were in their mid-50's and were purchasing a move-up home. However, the husband, while reviewing the HUD-1 settlement statement, was surprised by the amount of money he needed to close the home.

"This is nearly $10,000 more than you told me I needed when I filled out the loan application," he declared.

Bob looked back over the settlement statement and the instructions from the mortgage lender. "Well," he said, "the problem is that your debt was too high. The difference is that you need to pay off some debt in order to qualify for the loan."

"What debt?" The man questioned.

"Apparently, according to our credit records, you owe nearly $10,000 on three credit cards," he said. "I discussed this with your wife last week. The interest rate on the credit cards is very high. Actually, paying these off will save you a lot of money each month."

> *Life Lesson: Marriage is a Partnership. In order for it to be successful, you must both be honest and open.*

The man looked back at the settlement statement as his wife twitched nervously beside him. "I don't have any credit cards," he said, and then, looking straight at her, "I told you what would happen if you didn't stop spending money." Rising, he calmly punched her dead in the nose, knocking her unconscious. After that, signed the settlement papers while Bob carefully extricated himself from the conference room, called the police with the result that the husband was arrested as he left the conference room.

Later, I asked Bob why he didn't call the police immediately. He responded that we had a home seller that needed to sell, and it wasn't fair to that couple to cancel the settlement for this couple's issues.

A Pair of Wives

Husbands and wives have been known to hide all sorts of things from their spouses. In one case, a couple came into the office seeking to buy a home using the husband's VA eligibility. Some of the greatest mortgage programs are available only to veterans. These are, of course, called VA loans. Using the program, a veteran may actually purchase a home with no money down.

In order to obtain such a loan, the veteran has to provide a DD214, and the Veteran's Administration runs a search for eligibility.

We were confused when the certificate came back showing that his eligibility was severely limited because he *had* an outstanding VA loan. Bob Wilfinger called the veteran's wife and asked if they were moving from another property they had sold, and was told they had not; nor did they presently own a home.

Life Lesson: Sometimes one is better than two.

"It's probably just a mix-up," Bob said. "I'll call you back."

However, the eligibility problem was not a simple mix-up of name or social security number. More research discovered that the veteran owned a home an hour's drive north, and that he owned it with another wife. It turned out that he had married twice, without either wife knowing, and he was caught!

It turns out two is not always better than one.

The Skinny Dipping Clients

About ten years ago I had a pair of clients, who purchased a beautiful ranch home with a gorgeous in ground pool surrounded by a patio. The ranch home was set up so that a door from the family room opened up to the back yard and the pool, as did a door from the master bedroom suite. As soon as I saw the property, I knew instantly that this would be one of the primary reasons for the purchase since they had told me they loved it to entertain.

About four months after moving in, April called and told me that she and her husband needed to sell it. I couldn't understand what the problem could be, since they were so enamored with the property when they purchased it. Fearful that they were getting divorced, I stopped by, only to discover that apparently, one of the things that had attracted them to this house was the idea that they might be able to skinny dip in the back yard.

> *Life Lesson: Accept what you can't correct in life and learn to live with it. You'll be a much happier person!*

However, they found that on the first few occasions when they snuck out of their bedroom door in the middle of the night, the older neighbors next door would wait for them, and come out and watch them. Obviously, this upset them. They wanted a little fun, not to be the object of voyeurs' interest. But when they had had a privacy fence erected, the neighbors had a deck built which allowed them to continue to watch.

This, of course, erupted into an enormous feud between neighbors, which after a while the young couple could no longer bear. We resold the property for them, sadly at a loss, and they moved on to greener pastures.

Not Shannon

The husband of another couple, who scheduled an appointment to view a new house in the area, introduced his wife as Shannon, whereupon, she glared at him and saying, "Shannon is your ex wife's name, not mine!" She got back in the car.

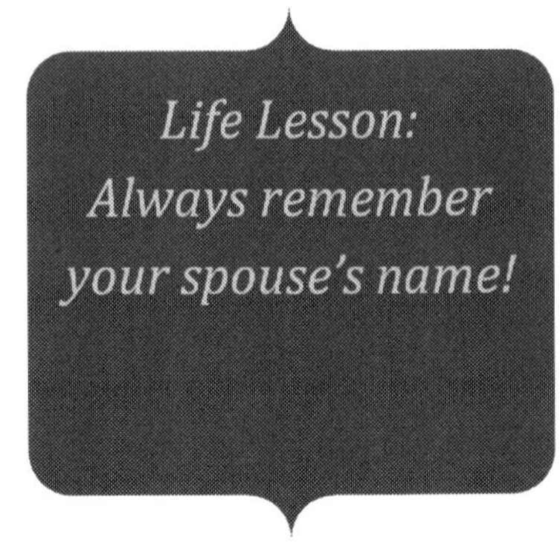

Shamefaced, he joined her and, I am afraid to say, I never saw them again.

Simply Ignore the Problem... Maybe it will go away!

One way to deal with problems is to just completely ignore them until it's too late to do anything about them. In one case, when we were contacted by a bank to take possession of a property in our market area, the bank representative explained to me that they had foreclosed on a town home in Whitehall, and that they wanted us, as representatives of the bank, to proceed with an eviction of the former owner, whom I had never met, who was still living there.

After sending a registered letter explaining that the home was now bank owned, and receiving no response, we filed an eviction order requiring the sheriff to serve the occupant with papers in order to force her from the property.

When, however, she did not show up at the hearing for the eviction, the judge set a date by which she would have to be out of her home. But despite a subsequent visit by the sheriff, she simply stayed where she was, a response that is all too frequent in cases like these.

The sheriff called me to make sure that I would be there at the date and time when she had to be forcibly removed, and I reluctantly agreed. Because of his tight schedule, the eviction was scheduled for December, shortly before Christmas. Appalled, my staff wanted to know whether or not I was going to kick a puppy on the way over to the house. However, I had no control over the legal system, no control over whether somebody does or does not pay their mortgage, and no control over what date the sheriff or the judge sets for such a removal but I was certainly not happy about all this.

When I got to the home, the occupant, a seventy plus year old widow, wanted to know what she would have to do to stay in the home. I explained that it was way too late now since the home had been foreclosed on several months earlier. The bank now owned the home, and the bank would not negotiate with her. They wanted her removed from the property, and the sheriff was there to lock her out, taking whatever she could pack quickly. She would have thirty days to collect the rest of her belongings.

She explained that her husband had passed away a few years earlier, leaving her enough in life insurance to pay off the mortgage, and a little bit to live on. But then, wanting to redecorate so that the home would not remind her so vividly of her husband, she had gone to a high risk loan company, borrowed enough money for the renovation project and enough money to buy presents for her three kids and her grand children. The entire equity loan had totaled at a little less than $20,000.

This had been the point at which she had failed to make mortgage payments, bringing the penalties and interest on top of the mortgage balance to somewhere in the neighborhood of $25,000. The home, at this point, was probably worth $135,000, and she could easily have sold it for $135,000, taken $100,000 in cash after paying off the mortgage and settlement charges, and lived comfortably for many years. Instead of confessing to her family that she was in trouble, she simply threw away the notices about nonpayment of the mortgage as she received them.

Sadly, many of us choose to avoid conflict or allow our pride to dictate our response to a bad situation. Instead of doing what is in our best interest, we allow ourselves to be ruled by the emotion of fear.

Please... Just Leave...

I had another situation several years earlier in which an owner was again choosing to ignore the ultimate consequences of foreclosure on her house. At one point in time, the home owners had been a well-to-do couple, having inherited from her father a fairly successful manufacturing company. Unfortunately, in the late 80's or early 90's, the textile industry had mostly moved overseas to take advantage of the less expensive work forces in China and Korea.

Life Lesson: Honesty begins with being honest to one-self.

The local company was unable to compete against the prices coming in from overseas, and the couple, being unwilling to outsource their own production to another country, chose to continue to employ local labor. Sadly, they ended up losing their company after nearly sixty years in business. Finally, in order to keep their family business going, they had mortgaged their house to the hilt, and now the bank was in the process of foreclosing on their last asset: the house.

The owners' attorney had stalled the bank by filing bankruptcy papers in order to keep the couple in the house for three years after they stopped paying the mortgage. However, the time was rapidly approaching when a sheriff's sale would result in there being physically removed from their home. When they finally came to me to try to sell the property, they were within weeks of being forcibly evicted from their home, and had no time to wait for the highest offer.

The market was slow and the average market time was in excess of ninety days, but they had less than sixty before they had to move. When I explained to them that we needed to price the home below market in order to get it sold in time, the wife became irate, saying that they needed every penny they could raise to pay off their debt. I explained to her, to the best of my ability, as I have to many home owners over time, that a home's sale price is a function of time. If you have all the time in the world to sell, you may get the highest possible price your property can command, but if you need to sell in a short period of time you may have to accept a wholesale price or below market price.

If we know that we only have a few weeks to sell a house, and there are fifty or sixty other comparable houses on the market, only two or three of them will sell in those few weeks. As a consequence, we have to make sure ours is the most attractive. After much discussion, we priced the house 10% below market and started an aggressive marketing campaign to try to get a sale before the sixty days were up.

After two weeks of attempting to attract buyers to view the property we were still receiving negative feedback about the owner's "dated" decor. I met with the owners to discuss lowering the price a little further. Again, we were on a tight time line. After the second price reduction, we were able to find a buyer who was able to close on the home very, very quickly, and was willing to pay their new lower price, but when I brought the sales contract over to their home, and went through the agreement with them, the wife was extremely unhappy, even though it was her only chance to solve their problem.

An argument ensued, one which ended with the wife running up the stairs, accusing her husband of making them lose their home because of having made poor business decisions. One of the most important lessons I've learned over time is that, unfortunately, people tend to blame the one closest to them for their financial misery, and it often is not the fault of the person closest to them.

There may be some poor decisions on someone's part, but the truth is it's very difficult to navigate the waters of an up and down economy, and changing competition in any field. After all, major companies with tens of thousands of employees, run by CEO's with Harvard MBA's, have gone bankrupt.

Her husband followed her up the steps, as I sat in the living room. They continued to argue on the second floor for nearly an hour. Not certain what to do, I remained steadfast on the sofa. Eventually he came back downstairs, asked me for the papers, and said that she was ready to sign but she would not come back downstairs because she was embarrassed. When he took them upstairs, I heard them arguing again, but in the end, they both signed. In fact, before I left, the wife apologized.

It wasn't just the loss of the home, she explained. She couldn't bear the thought of losing her family business and leaving the family home. For year, she had taken walks in the neighborhood daily, and walked down to the park to relax. Of course, she loved the home and hated to walk away from it, and she couldn't believe, she said, that she was selling it at what she considered to be such a low price.

One of the other things I've learned over the years, working with thousands of people, is that nearly everyone believes their home is the best in an area for some reason, and therefore, that it is worth more than the others in the area. And they believe it should sell for a little bit more.

On the day of settlement the sellers signed all of the papers, but then came the surprise – the wife decided to barricade herself in the home. The buyers called me, irate, and I stopped over to see the buyers' moving truck in the driveway, the seller screaming out the window and refusing to come out of the house, her husband's standing in the driveway apologizing, and everyone's attorneys arguing. After nearly three hours of battling back and forth, we were able to coax her out of the house, complete the transaction and allow the buyers to move in.

The other truth I learned from this story, which has been repeated over and over again, is that the end is never truly the end. Several months later I received a phone call from an attorney. I always enjoy these phone calls because too many attorneys seem to grasp at anything humanly possible to begin a lawsuit in order to make some money for themselves or their client, and often wonder if we would not be performing a service if we made the losing party in any frivolous lawsuit pay the full freight of the legal fees.

This particular attorney said that he was now representing my former client who claimed that she had been deliberately forced out of her home at a low point in the real estate market and that, furthermore, this had happened in order to comply with an agreement of sale that she never really signed.

According to the attorney, the former owner claimed that she had gone into the hospital with a nervous condition on the day the agreement was signed. She believed that I came to visit her in the hospital with the sales contract, and while she was not completely conscious, I had taken her hand and forged her name with it. I almost laughed. I explained to the attorney how ludicrous that was.

If I were attempting to forge a document, I certainly wouldn't need to go to the hospital and use her hand. Secondly, she wasn't in the hospital at the time, and third, she was just days away from being physically removed from the property by the Sheriff, so he had no case.

Her attorney asked if I would consider offering a settlement in order to avoid all the bad publicity he and his client would dredge up. After all, he explained, using a favorite tactic of these legal master-minds, this was a helpless older woman forced from her home. A protracted lawsuit would cost me tens of thousands of dollars and a loss of good will in the community.

"Absolutely not," I said. "I'll be happy to see you in Court." That was the last I heard from him.

Home Pricing Strategies

People seem to live so much of their lives on an emotional rather than a logical level. In my experience, not only do more than nine out of ten home owners that I meet with to sell a property honestly believe that their home is worth more than the market dictates, many of them believe that if we use some magical marketing program, the home will sell for a greater price.

Just this week I encountered another home seller who was unhappy with my rational and realistic view of the market. Art and Jeanine were relocating to Texas and needed to make "everything possible" out of the house in order to make the move. After all, the market in the northeast had been down, but the San Antonio market was doing fine, and they wanted to be able to make an even trade.

This was a relatively easy home to price because it was a four bedroom, two and a half bath colonial built only a few years ago in a large neighborhood of similar homes.

In the past few months, the home next door to Art and Jeanine's, which was identical to theirs, had just sold for $360,000. That sale alone can help us to set the most likely sales price of the property, because it indicated what recent buyers were willing to pay for a home like theirs. Another home, a block away was listed at $355,000, and has been on the market for seven months, and again, was virtually identical to Art and Jeanine's.

A home a block in the other direction which was also very similar was on the market for $359,900, and had not sold in nearly a year and a half, because the market had slowed. Buyers determine what they're willing to pay for homes based on looking at twelve to fifteen competing properties.

Even if we are able to convince a buyer to pay a premium, the lender is likely to reject the loan after an appraisal is done. We can always shoot for the sky, but we have to be prepared to accept the harsh reality of the marketplace.

When I told them that their property would probably sell very close to that of the neighbor's house, Jeanine was immediately offended.

"We want $390,000, and we're not going to give our house away. If we have to, we'll sit on it for the next several years".

When I replied that I had I understood that they were relocating within several weeks, she said, "That's true, but I will just hold the house until the market improves".

My response, of course, was that her mortgage payment was probably close to $3,000 a month, and that, as a consequence, it would cost approximately $36,000 a year to hold onto the house.

"It doesn't matter," she replied. "I am not giving this house away."

This was a highly educated woman who understood math and something of economics, and yet still talked to me on an emotional level about her home's value.

When we're pricing houses, we all have to understand that they are commodities, nothing else, and prices of commodities go up and go down. If you bought a share of Google stock at $400, and it's now trading at $200 a share, it doesn't matter how well you advertise it, you will not sell it for $400 a share, because it's a commodity.

Although every house is a little unique, the truth is that if you have a four bedroom, two and a half bath colonial in a neighborhood of four bedroom, two and a half bath colonials, and there are ten for sale, buyers will look at a dozen of them, and make an informed decision.

Throw in the Garden Hose

A few years ago, I accompanied one of our associate brokers, Tim Mahon, on a listing appointment to look at a townhome in Allentown, the pricing of which would be relatively easy because several had recently sold in the neighborhood. The owner, Randy, met us at the front door and walked through the home, noting that it was fairly typical of the townhomes in the neighborhood. But when Tim

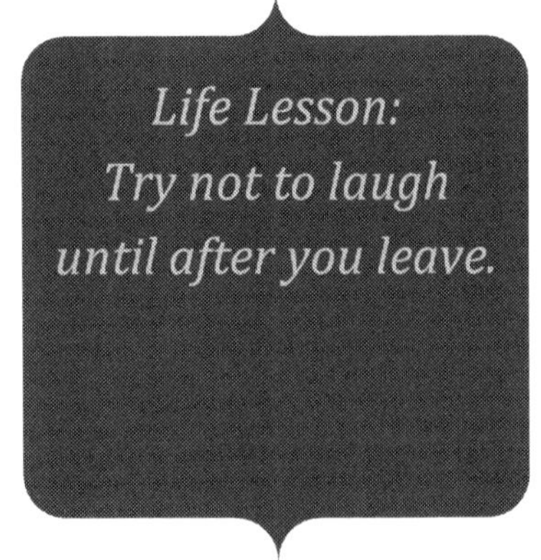

explained that the house would likely sell very close in price to the next door neighbors, Randy's mood changed.

He was offended that we would "even compare" his home with his neighbors. "My home is worth at least $25,000 more than his. Do you realize that the neighbor's home still has all the rooms painted white? Mine has color! And the neighbor has regular closet bars. I had Creative Closets put in double racks in PVC. Also, I had a hose bib put on both the front and back of my home. The neighbor only had one put on the back. Plus, I'm planning to throw in the twenty-five foot garden hose."

Tim actually lost it at that point. "The garden hose is included?" he exclaimed, laughing hysterically. "Wow. That's got to be worth $5,000 to $10,000 in price. Why don't we list this house $40,000 higher than the neighbors if you're throwing in the garden hose?"

Needless to say, we didn't get the listing.

Preserving Child Custody

Not all stories end badly. Wayne Taliber, an agent with our Allentown office, worked with the Farmer's Home Loan agency to get one of our clients into a home in under thirty days in order to comply with a judge's order. Apparently, because there was no longer a mother in the picture, and the father had been unable to keep a permanent residence for the prior two years, a judge had ordered him to actually purchase a home within thirty days in order to prove that he could provide a stable environment for his son. If he failed to secure a home and produce evidence of settlement, the child would be taken from him and placed into the foster care system.

With less than stellar credit, a buyer is limited to purchasing a home with a significant down payment or resorting to a federal loan program that allows the buyer to explain their situation.

Wayne found that the only program Stephen could qualify for, based on his minimal cash situation and shaky credit, was the Farmer's Home Loan program. At the time, this particular program only accepted very specific types of homes and home locations in rural areas. Additionally, although there has been a dramatic improvement in the system recently, processing of this type of loan often ran more than sixty days. Farmer's Home put the loan together without a fee in order to keep the closing costs in line with what Stephen needed in order to settle.

Working diligently, Stephen secured a contract to purchase a home, and Farmer's Home pushed the loan through their departments at light speed.

At closing, on the 29th day, Stephen found he was short a few hundred dollars. Everyone at the table *found* money to assist him in meeting the deadline to keep his son.

The Pusher, the Kids and the Gun

There seems to be drug trafficking even in the quietest of areas. Sadly, too many people seek an escape from their lives or their reality by way of substance abuse which often becomes the tool of the user's own destruction.

On a cool autumn afternoon in my old neighborhood, I found that a teenage supplier was giving away samples, stickers that could be licked to produce a high, to elementary school age kids. My guess was that the pusher was trying to either make them habitual or addicted users.

In either case, I was irate. Being somewhat irrational when angry, I proceeded to find the teenage pusher and show him the error of his ways in ways that are unnecessary to describe here. After all, there may be small children and nuns reading this book. Anyway, I was confident, after our little talk, that the pusher would never set foot in the neighborhood again, for fear of being permanently maimed.

Fast forward a few weeks. My friend and real estate associate, Joe Bartera, and I stopped, on our way to an appointment, at a Seven Eleven for a couple of sodas. We were driving a Dodge Monaco, which was a former state police car that I had purchased at an auction in Harrisburg. The car had a roll cage and was made of real steel rather than the plastic that automobiles seem to be made with today. Of course, it got the gas mileage of a tractor trailer with a full load, a dirty filter, and dragging two deer, but I digress.

Life Lesson: Always think before you act. Your actions may have unintended consequences for you and for those around you.

Stepping out of the car, I had neglected to tell Joe that the passenger side lock didn't work, and then, remembering, I called out, "Don't lock your door."

"Too late," he said as the door slammed. "It's locked and besides, my mother always told me to lock the car, even in nice safe neighborhoods."

When we were leaving the Seven Eleven minutes later, sodas in hand, a full size sedan pulled up at a "T" behind my car and the drug pushing teenager that I had a chat with some time before popped out of the car, followed, more laboriously, by a large contingent of enormous gentlemen.

"That's him," he said, pointing at me. .

"Crap," I said, realizing they probably weren't stopping by to congratulate me on my good works on behalf of society. Leaping into the driver's side of the car, I started the engine and attempted to slam the door.

Joe dropped the soda and ran for the car only to discover that the lock didn't open. Frantically, he began yelling obscenities that had never before crossed his Catholic lips, while I, managing to pop the lock and put the car into drive, waited for him to leap in. It was the sort of stunt you would probably never be able to pull off twice.

The goon who was closest to my door, as I floored the accelerator going forward away from the car blocking my path behind, had on what appeared to be brass knuckles. "Wow, I didn't think those things really existed," I vividly recall thinking as the car spun to the left toward the exit to the mini mart where another goon ran in front of the car and took aim with a gun. "A gun?" I thought. "Oh crap."

More obscenities streamed from the passenger side of my car as this enormous man fired a single shot right between us just before I hit him with the car.

"Are you okay?" I shouted at Joe as we peeled out of the parking lot at high speed. When he didn't respond, I glanced over at him and saw that he was white as a ghost, which was highly unusual for this typically tan Italian, but he didn't appear to be spraying blood in any particular direction. That was good. I was fairly certain blood wouldn't come out of the seat coverings.

Rather than take him to the hospital which I should have done, I took him to a nearby home of a friend, by which time, Joe had gone into shock. Once he had recovered, we debated calling the police and eventually decided against it, although we had been violently attacked, it was also true that I hit the man, almost certainly causing at least some bodily damage. And that did not even take into consideration the fact that I had roughed up the fellow who was supplying drugs to the local youth.

I also rationalized that the odds were good that the teenager didn't actually know who I was or exactly where I lived, so if I were to report the crime and identify myself, the entire cartel could be after me.

Prior to that incident, the likelihood that a teenager pushing drugs would have a supply chain that would protect him had never occurred to me. After that night, thankfully, I was never bothered by them again, although I often looked over my shoulders for probably three or four years.

My mistake, looking back, was that I hadn't handled the original situation correctly. I should have reported it to the authorities and I certainly should have talked to the kid's parents and tried to help them without taking action into my own hands. I guess I read too many Shadow Novels and Batman Comics as a kid. Of course, I still love Batman. Who doesn't?

Incidentally, Joe didn't get in a car with me for nearly ten years after that episode. On the bright side, he's still working with me today.

Chapter 3:
Half of the World is Crazy… The Other Half is Plain Nuts

As realtors, we never quite know what kind of situation we're going to find ourselves in until it's too late. A few years ago, I was called to estimate the value of the home of a couple who were divorcing. Stepping onto the porch, I discovered that someone had nailed a doll to the door, and made it more graphic, not only by sticking a nail through its neck but by streaking the body of the doll, as well as the front of the door, with red paint. People never fail to surprise me.

Pat, a real estate agent who had worked with me in the Allentown, Pennsylvania office of our firm, regularly joked that we *really* needed to stop advertising in *Psycho Buyers Today*. After working with the public for more than two decades, I've come to realize that there are *lots* of people in this world that, despite their apparent ability to function in their everyday life seem, in reality, downright crazy. Of course, making such a statement will probably net me hundreds of letters from mental health care advocates and professionals who feel I am insensitive, but I've always preferred to be blunt (and lighten up – it's a joke).

I first realized the pervasiveness of the sort of insanity to which I'm referring more than twenty years ago when, together with some friends of mine, I took fifty or sixty teenagers camping. Actually, looking back, it was insanity for my group to think we could actually handle fifty or sixty teenagers in the woods. However, we had gone on this outing several times before. On this particular occasion, we brought along a young man named Roger.

On the first evening of the campout, we traditionally built a large fire, and sat around it, roasting marshmallows and telling stories about former campers whose bodies, for a variety of reasons, had never been fished out of the nearby lake and whose ghosts continued to haunt the grounds nightly, showing a special interest in teenagers. These tales were, as we expected, greeted by our friends and charges with shrieks and shudders.

On the second and final evening, our plan was to light an equally large bonfire, and since the ash and a small amount of remaining wood was still smoldering in the middle of our fire pit, I proceeded to build a large pyre over top of the ashes by standing large logs against each other. Although we didn't intend to officially light the fire until later that night, I didn't believe the logs would catch from the remaining embers.

Roger, however, with trickery in mind, having filled a plastic cup with kerosene or propane, sneaked up behind me while I was bent over the pit and dumped the flammable liquid on the embers, causing an upsurge of flames that rapidly removed most of my eyebrows.

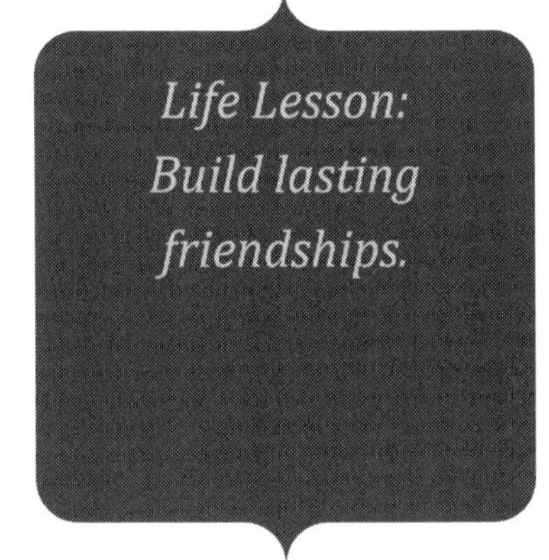

Friends of mine, Tom LaDue and Todd Siegfried, hung Roger upside down from a tree for several hours after that. In the current environment, this would probably have resulted in their being arrested or, at the very least, sued. But at the time, they felt this was an appropriate response to Roger's attempt to flame broil me, and I agree. Punishments need to fit the crimes.

Subconsciously, I believe far too many of us really want to hurt ourselves or see someone else hurt. Others seem to have a sense of invulnerability. For example, the husband of an employee at our title company recently decided to dramatically show what crazy really means.

Her husband decided to trim a tree out front with a chainsaw. Unfortunately, the ladder didn't quite reach high enough to get at the offending limbs. In a moment of sheer brilliance, he drove his van up to the tree and put on the emergency brake and, when that didn't work either, actually set up a ladder on the roof of the vehicle, on a hill, from which vantage point, he proceeded to operate the chainsaw. Thankfully he didn't dismember himself, but I don't think it was for a lack of trying.

The Cloistered Nuns and the Monastery

The president of a very successful large corporation built an expansive Mediterranean style home next to a large monastery just north of the famously expensive Bucks County. The home featured every conceivable luxury available at the time it was built including automatic towel warmers in the bathrooms and inlaid mahogany in the hardwood flooring. A circular driveway brought visitors under roof to disembark from their cars for the posh social gatherings held in the home and there was also a state-of-the-art bomb shelter for protection against our cold war enemies, fully stocked with food, water and the necessities of life.

Some time later, the successful businessman and his wife began arguing, with the result that they divided the home in half, one side for the husband and one side for the wife, each with its own master suite and areas to entertain, and lived that way for several years. At some point, however, the police were called because the wife had vanished.

Arriving at their happy home, the police noted that the bomb shelter had been filled in, and although the husband suggested that his estranged wife had simply run off, she had, inexplicably enough, left her clothing, her personal belongings and even her car behind. A cursory investigation followed, during which the bomb shelter was never opened. The businessman, who had significant clout in the area, was never charged with any crime.

This is the story that Al, the most recent owner of the property, told me when I met with him to list his property for sale. For some reason which seemed to have escaped him, he had never opened the bomb shelter to see whether or not they were harboring a body.

But that might not be the most interesting story about this unique property. The monastery next door, surrounded by high walls on every side, was home to a sect of cloistered nuns, who lived such secluded lives that, according to rumor, event the priests, when they came to give communion, administered it through a veil.

> *Life Lesson:*
> *Accept each life*
> *experience as an*
> *opportunity to learn*
> *something of value.*

At all events, while marketing the unique Mediterranean home, I discovered that, off one of the master suites, a lovely second story balcony overlooked the monastery walls, providing a view not only of its orchards and gardens, but the activities of several of the nuns who appeared to be riding something that looked like a giant tricycle. How odd, I thought as I left.

By the time I returned to my office, there was a message waiting for me from the Mother Superior. Returning her call, I found that she was irate because the nuns required complete privacy. To this end, she forbid me or anyone who viewed the home to use the balcony. I explained that I had no control over what the new owners would or would not do, and suggested that perhaps she should plant tall trees. She would hear nothing of the sort. No one, she repeated, was to use that balcony.

Always careful to make full disclosure, I conveyed all this information to the interested party who, to my astonishment, seemed to have no problem with it, and purchased the home. In fact, they were apparently so lacking in curiosity in regard to the bomb shelter that, as far as I know, it has not been opened to this day.

I'm thinking of calling Geraldo Rivera.

The Blue Magic Marker

Wayne Taliber and I arrived in the small borough of Catasauqua to possibly list a property for sale, the right side of a townhouse owned by a potential client named Kay who had been a nurse for nearly twenty years.

As she opened the door to admit us, our eyes began to fill with water, not because we had suddenly begun to weep but because we were overcome by the noxious odor of cat pee. Cats seldom bother me, and I am certainly not allergic to them, but in this case, Kay's five male cats had apparently gone on a spraying spree. "You know how boys are!" she said, which was very little consolation, given the fact that this would inevitably be the smell that would welcome potential buyers.

The next thing that struck me was that everything was pink, the walls, the ceiling, the carpeting and even the drapes. Actually, everything was pink *except* for two doors and the molding for the opening to the second floor staircase, all of which were painted white, a pristine surface on which, inexplicably, someone had scribbled an unintelligible message in blue magic marker, which continued to zigzag its way up the staircase.

"I'm so sorry," she said, no doubt struck by my appalled expression. "I have a two year old and you know how they can be. I turned my back on him for just a few minutes and magic marker was everywhere," which was an extraordinary claim, considering the molding over the landing was more than six feet off the floor.

"So, your two year old got hold of a ladder?" My companion, Wayne, remarked dryly.

Later, Kay admitted that she really loved pink, and her husband, knowing they were planning on selling the home, had decided to neutralize the colors, by repainted the two doors and molding white while she was away. She was, she explained, so angry with him that she had had recourse to her revenge via a blue magic marker.

It never fails to astonish me how we, as people, seem to be so completely controlled by our basest emotions. I'm hoping never to have her as a nurse, should I be hospitalized, or at least not anger her while I'm a patient.

> *Life Lesson: Resolve conflicts quickly. Letting them build and fester leads to greater problems.*

Speaking of nurses, one of our agents, who I'll call Lynn, was hospitalized for a condition that required surgery. When she returned to the office, everyone gathered around to ask how she was feeling and someone added, "Were you scared?"

"Well," Lynn said, "I was a little scared about the surgery, but there was one thing that terrified me as I was going under the anesthesia."

"What?" we all asked together.

"Well, you remember my telling you that I had dated someone in my old career, before I went into real estate. He was in the process of leaving his wife at the time. Anyway, as the anesthesiologist was placing the mask over me, she looked at my face and demanded to know if I was the same Lynn Babson who had slept with her husband."

That was not, she assured me, precisely what anyone wants to hear just before going "under the knife." And I must admit that I had to agree.

Mrs. P and the Bagel Part 1

People have varying levels of comfort as far as cleanliness is concerned. Unfortunately, each person has their own view of what is clean and what is not. For example, I can't tell you the number of individuals I've met that share their meals with their pets. No, I'm not talking about dropping a scrap of meat under the table for Bowzer, the family dog. I'm talking about sharing a sandwich with your pet, one bite at a time.

While I hope not to offend those of you in my reading audience who are truly animal lovers, I find that to be outright gross. Yes, I have heard that a dog's mouth is cleaner than ours, but I don't really care. I don't share my sandwiches with other people either.

I met Mrs. P and her children when I visited her home in South Allentown. I'm not really certain how many children she had, because they were in such constant motion running about the home, and because my attention was caught by a number of significant cobwebs hanging from the ceiling and some really, really dirty, not to mention sticky, floors littered with a variety of food particles including cheerios, green peas and less identifiable substances.

Then Mrs. P stopped me cold by saying, "You shouldn't have a problem selling *this* house. After all, this is one of the cleanest homes you will ever see. I work my fingers to the bone keeping this home in order."

Now, let me be perfectly honest. I've seen people fool themselves into believing all sorts of crazy things, but this was outright denial. When she ushered me into the kitchen, I was amazed to see a rather large dog which might or might not have been a Labrador, licking food particles off the table, and although she shooed him away, there was so much food, including generous dollops of jelly, remaining that I didn't dare to put my writing tablet there, and was forced to prop it on my knee.

"I'll fix you a bagel," she announced, selecting one from a wire bowl in the center of the table.

"Ok." I responded reluctantly. Over the years, I've taken several sales courses in which we were told a customer would be more comfortable with a salesperson if they accepted whatever was offered, a consultative approach which I have long since adopted. However, in this case, the thought of eating anything in this dubiously hygienic environment was definitely not appealing. As she was already slapping cream cheese on a bagel which she had severed with what appeared to be a rusty knife, I could, I found, think of nothing to say. The idea of faking a cream cheese allergy didn't occur to me until after I had left.

I watched, appalled, as she licked her fingers before picking up the bagel, and then, to top it off, set it down, sans plate, on the

> *Life Lesson: Each of us have a perception or a paradigm about our lives and surroundings. Our reality is defined by that perception.*

already obscured surface of the table. It was a tough decision as to whether or not any home listing could be worth eating that bagel.

Mrs. P Part 2

Yes, I listed Mrs. P's home for sale. Don't ask me why. And surprisingly enough, eventually, we even received an offer on it, although, as it turned out, that was only the beginning of our difficulties since the house was in her husband's name, and he, quite understandably, wanted to review the offer documents, which should have been simple enough had it not been for the fact that his wife appeared every few minutes to demand that he perform some menial task, which he, apparently well trained, consistently leaped to his feet to obey.

What should have taken about twenty minutes to explain had now run into a second full hour. He would sit down across from me, I would get half a sentence out, and she would reappear with another request. At one point, she actually came in and asked him to make dinner for the children. I kid you not.

When settlement was ultimately scheduled for the property, our title agent, Gwyn, called and asked what was up with this crazy woman.

"What's the problem?" I asked her.

"She's calling us every fifteen minutes with one question at a time," Gwyn told me. "We can't get any work done."

I promised that, if she continued to be a problem, I would buy the staff lunch. And since she continued to call repeatedly for the next two weeks, that was precisely what I had to do.

At settlement, Mr. and Mrs. P arrived with their attorney and Mrs. P's father, the lady promptly announcing that her husband would not sign a single paper until the attorney had read, "every single word." The groan that rose from us sitting around the table was certainly an understandable response, given that loan documentation is not only written in legalese, but can also be a few inches thick. Requiring someone to read through all this is akin to water boarding and would, no doubt, be considered torture by the World Court.

After nearly an hour of reading through the documentation, Mrs. P's attorney proclaimed it to be acceptable, whereupon Mrs. P picked up the pile of papers and handed them to her father. "I want them double checked, Daddy," she said. "Please read through these." My jaw dropped and the settlement agent dropped her calculator and left the room.

To top it off, after her father had also agreed that the paperwork was, indeed, in order, she moved the stack of papers to her husband with the same instructions. The groans were much louder this time, and when the buyer left the room, he shut the door with a bang.

"Mrs. P," I said in a conciliatory voice, "the paperwork is the same that we use for every closing. There is nothing wrong with it and you have an attorney's opinion that there is nothing wrong with it. We need to get this wrapped up."

"This is a very important decision," she rebuked me indignantly, "and we need to make certain that all the I's are dotted and the T's are crossed."

The house, by the way, sold for less than $100,000 and for their troubles in this transaction, I bought the title staff lunch at the most expensive Italian restaurant in the area. Sometimes we simply need to walk away from a client. There are times that a sale simply isn't worth the aggravation.

Theresa and the Lemonade

My wife Theresa accompanied me on a listing appointment in a beautiful suburban neighborhood in Macungie. On the drive to the home, Theresa complained that she was really thirsty. As we turned onto Route 100 South, I saw several mini-markets, but since we were already late for the appointment, I asked if she really wanted me to stop, and she replied that it was better to get to the appointment. I pointed out that most of my listing appointments run more than an hour, but she assured me that she'd be fine.

As soon as we were seated at the dining room table, the property owner, a gracious hostess, asked us if she could get us anything, "Perhaps," she suggested, "a glass of lemonade?"

"No thanks." Theresa responded. "I'm fine." Theresa is an extraordinary person, but she's also someone who typically refuses anything offered. I think this is something ingrained from childhood.

Life Lesson: Accepting gifts graciously can make both the given and the receiver feel good.

"I'd love a glass." I said, following the dictum that, as I mentioned before, the salesperson should always accept what is offered.

Amy, the owner, poured a glass for me and one for herself before turning to set the pitcher back on the buffet across from the table, providing my wife with the opportunity to grab my glass of lemonade and down most of it in one amazingly quick slurp, occasioning a comment regarding the extent of my thirst which, with my usual command of witty responses, I replied by saying that yes, indeed, I had been parched.

Understanding Engineers

As anyone in sales knows, the most challenging prospects are generally those individuals who overanalyze situations. There are many engineers and accountants who fall into this category, as well as people with OCD. Those who are technically oriented may be highly intelligent, but they may also be working primarily out of one side of their brain. Please don't misunderstand me. I have an engineering background. My grandfather was a very successful engineer in his time, and in college, I majored in electrical engineering. Some engineers, however, can drive us absolutely bonkers in the sales business.

> *Life Lesson: Each of us has strengths and weaknesses. Recognize your own strengths as well as those in others.*

Many engineers tend to be very methodical and very precise, making sure that every little detail is managed properly. I've had some engineers call me ten or more times each day to double check on the details of a transaction. Unfortunately, when someone calls me that often, I can't concentrate on getting any work done. I've also had many engineers, some accountants, and some other individuals, sit at settlement and actually read, word for word, every document the mortgage company sends them to sign. Of course, unlike Mrs. P, these professionals generally only read the papers once. As I mentioned earlier, if you've never bought a house, there is a lot of paperwork from mortgage companies at settlement, and reading word for word can take hours and turn a forty-five minute closing into an all day event.

An attorney at one of the settlements I attended delivered one of my favorite lines to an engineering client when he asked what a specific clause in a mortgage document meant. After reading and rereading the clause, he announced, "I have no idea, but it doesn't really matter because if you don't sign it they won't give you the mortgage, and you won't close on the house, and you won't be moving in today."

My first experience with one of these very methodical thinkers took place when I was showing houses to an engineer who had just relocated into the area to work for Air Products and Chemicals. The first showing took nearly three hours, during which he made to scale sketches of every room, including closets, and took such copious notes that, by the time we left, he had filled an entire notebook.

"You must really love this house." I said, hopefully, thinking he *must* love the house since he had spent so much time detailing every aspect of it.

"No. I'm actually not really that crazy about it," he told me, "but I wanted to be able to remember it after leaving."

"Oh." I said, surprised by this unfortunate turn, and truly perplexed by his insistence on diagramming a home that he didn't have a strong feel for.

When it came to the second house, he looked at the living room which was very dated, with an older fireplace, chipping plaster walls, and hardwood floors which needed to be repaired, and said, "This is not the house for me".

"No problem," I said, "we can leave now. I'll make apologies to the owner."

"Actually, I'd still like to look at the property," he said and proceeded to spend four hours sketching and writing down detailed notes about the entire property. Several times during this ridiculously long showing, I asked him if he had changed his mind, or if, perhaps, this might be a house he would be interested in.

And even though he assured me that this was not the house for him, he, inexplicably enough, continued sketching rooms and taking notes.

Eventually, I did sell him a house, although, in the process, it frequently occurred to me that, he would, I'm sure, have tried the patience of a saint.

Stalking Our Buyers

Many realtors instruct their clients that they should be gone from the home during showings, on the basis that the buyer will have difficulty viewing the home as *theirs* if the owner is present, to emotionally connect, if you will. Also, as I mentioned in an earlier story, a home seller can talk themselves out of the sale if we're not careful.

A few months after my first encounter with a *true* engineer, I had a call from another one, a man who needed to sell his home in order to relocate. He was, I soon discovered, the proud possessor of several patents for various inventions, and although single, a compulsive clean freak who, for the purpose of our showings, had installed plastic runners everywhere, and requested that my assistant and I remove our shoes outside the door.

While I was explaining how I intended to go about showing the house, I mentioned that it might be a good idea for him to vamoose during viewings, in response he explained that he couldn't leave because he had too many secret designs located throughout the house. He was so sure that his work could be compromised if he weren't present that reluctantly, we gave in.

For the next two weeks, my assistant received odd calls from agents who had shown the property, complaining about the seller's strange behavior. Apparently, not only was he at home for every showing, but he insisted on following the potential buyers through the house. One of them, it seemed, had complained to my assistant about being stalked.

"Stalked?" I said. "You must have misheard. If he's following people through the home, I'll try to talk him out of it, but *stalking?*"

I called Stan and explained that if he had to be home, it might be a good idea to stay in one area while the realtor shows the buyers through the home. "Please don't follow them." I asked and he agreed.

During the second week of the listing, we held an open house and discovered the problem my fellow agents were having. Stan greeted us, wearing rubber gloves, and of course, each visitor had to remove their shoes. As we walked through the home, Stan, equipped with a spray bottle and rag, stayed just out of sight, but as soon as we left a room, he would emerge to wipe the door knobs and anything he believed we had touched.

When the house finally sold – which miraculously it did – I had to wonder if the buyer had the same odd compulsive behaviors as the seller. If so, I certainly hope that he does not come to us when he puts the place on the market.

A Little Piece of History

"Mr. Keim, I've recently read a magazine article that says you're an expert in the value of historic homes," a caller recently asked.

"Well, I don't know if there's any such thing as a *real* expert," I replied, "but I've sold quite a few farmhouses, log homes and Victorian era homes. I understand the market, if that's what you mean."

After assuring me numerous times that what he needed was an expert opinion, we scheduled a meeting. In order to be thoroughly prepared, I pulled the tax records on the property and noted that he had purchased the house less than two years before. As a result, therefore, of the market having been so stagnant lately, and his assurance on the phone that he had made no significant renovations, I assumed that the price would be much the same as it had been when he purchased it, which would have put it at $325,000.

The stone farmhouse was located in a popular school district and next to a park, which was promising. However, one of the first things I noted when I went inside was that the hardwood floors had been painted gray.

"I painted them gray to keep in character with the historic qualities of the home," the owner told me.

I had been selling historic homes for over a decade at this point in my career, and having never seen anyone actually paint over beautiful historic wide plank hardwood flooring, I was flabbergasted.

Chase went on to describe all the wonderful things he had done to the home since purchasing it two years earlier, none of which, as far as I could see, had added any value to it whatsoever, while rooms that could have benefitted from a bit of improvement seemed to have had nothing done to them. The bedrooms were small, and lacking closets, which was consistent with the period, but a difficult sale in modern society.

As for the basement, it was in its original condition, damp, dingy and low ceilinged, requiring us to stoop while viewing lest we risk damaging head injuries. Strangely enough, the basement sported a brick floor, something that I had never before seen.

"A member of the DuPont family," Chase said, clearing his throat, "was here to visit me. I'm very close to the family. Seeing this unique brick floor, he got down on his knees, kissed the floor, and said that he would pay me a million dollars for this home on that day if only I'd agree to sell it to him immediately. Homes with this type of brick floor are rare in any part of the original colonies."

Of course, I immediately became quite concerned. Although I

> *Life Lesson:*
> *Try to look at every situation logically. People can delude themselves into believing anything that is in their self interest.*

seriously doubted any member of the DuPont family actually offered the owner such a ridiculously high sum for a three hundred thousand dollar home meant that the owner most likely had some unrealistic expectations of the likely sales price of the home. But there's a lot of self delusion in this world. People can convince themselves of the craziest things. "Wow, that's a really great price." I said. "I probably would have sold it to him if I were you."

"At that point, I was planning to stay here for many years, so I wouldn't sell," he told me. "My plans have changed."

"Well, before we do anything, I'd suggest you try to get hold of your friend and determine if he still has an interest in this house. He's probably your best buyer."

After a bit of hemming and hawing, however, he explained that his DuPont friend had gone on to bigger and better things.

We returned to the kitchen table, and the long list of recent sales of farmhouses was on top. The highest price of a farmhouse recently sold in the area was less than $400,000. "Ordinarily, I begin to explain how I market properties, where I position them, and how I determine the most likely sales price of a property." I said. "But I really don't think I'm the realtor for you."

"Why would you think that?" he demanded. "You come very highly recommended and I'm looking for the best."

"Well, it comes down to this," I said. "I believe your expectations are significantly higher than the price I think the property can possibly be sold for."

"Don't be so concerned," he insisted. "You can tell me anything you want to as long as you're honest. You could tell me this home is worth $200,000, and if you're being honest, I won't be upset. I just want your professional opinion as to what the value of the house is in today's market. Now I have a number in mind, but I'm curious as to where you see it being positioned."

"Okay," I said, and went on to explain that the majority of stone farmhouses in the area at that point in time were selling between $250,000 and $350,000 and although his home had a slight edge in that it was next to a park and in a popular school district, there were many features of the property that needed some cosmetic work, including re-sanding the floors to expose the hardwood and remove the paint."

"Price-wise, I see you in the neighborhood of $350,000, "I told him which was, in my opinion, a generous figure.

His response, however, was to leap to his feet and shout, "Get out! Get out! It's obvious that you know absolutely nothing about historic houses. This place is unique. To market it for less than a million would be a great giveaway. Furthermore, you're an idiot…"

And on, and on.

I collected my things and hurried out of the house, with him trailing me, shouting obscenities. In the end, he listed the property with one of my competitors for just under $800,000, and it came as no surprise to me that it sat on the market for several years without selling.

Holiday Showings

The real estate market moves differently around the country, but in the colder regions the primary marketing seasons tend to be the spring and the fall. In most parts of the country, real estate sales tend to slow down around the holidays. The market becomes sluggish the week before Thanksgiving and doesn't begin recovering until after New Years. The slowest week of the year is often that week before Christmas when much of America is running around buying last minute gifts, or if you're in my family, just beginning to shop.

This year, I received a very angry call from one of our home sellers only a few days before Christmas. "Loren, have I not expressed to you how important it is to get my home sold as soon as possible?"

"I realize that you need to get the home sold," I told him. We just put a great ad in the local homes magazine and updated the video tour on the Internet."

"Then why do we have no showings scheduled for this weekend?" he demanded.

"I'm not sure that I understand you," I said. "It's only a few days before Christmas."

"That's right, and I don't have a showing. Something needs to be done about it right away."

"You have to understand that there are about five thousand homes on the market in your area right now," I told him. "Five thousand families are trying to sell their homes this week and there are probably only a half dozen buyers actually looking during the holiday."

But he remained unconvinced, apparently under the impression that we realtors have a list of people just waiting to buy anything that comes on the market, and I was reminded, once again, that one of the most interesting aspects of human nature is that we can fool ourselves into believing almost anything.

Cash Buyers

Early in my career, I listed a bicycle shop for sale. A pair of Korean gentlemen, who spoke very poor English, viewed the property and made a cash offer with a quick settlement. The owner of the bicycle shop was thrilled. Small cash businesses are often difficult to finance because commercial lenders require significant down payments, as well as proof of the business's cash flow, with the result that the owners often waffle about their true profits.

A few weeks later, we met for settlement at a local title insurance company. After signing the necessary paperwork, the title agent requested the cashier's check for the balance of the purchase. The first buyer explained they had brought cash, and proceeded to pull tens of thousands of dollars in bills out of their pants where, it seems, they had stored it in the waistbands of their underwear. There are times when even I won't touch money.

In the US, we are not permitted to take cash of $10,000 or above without complete records of where it's coming from, so it came as no surprise that this was the first occasion I had ever seen someone try to pay cash for a property. The title agent refused the money and asked them to go to a bank, report the money and bring back a cashier's check.

I guess you never quite know what's down someone's pants.

Telephone Solicitation

One of our agents that sold real estate on a part time basis showed several in-town properties to a young woman who claimed to be able to put twenty percent down. At the time, that was unusual for urban homes. At each showing, the woman was accompanied by several men.

Then, after selecting the home she wanted, came back to our office to write an offer. As our agent completed the paperwork, he asked for a deposit check. The buyer pulled out an old paper bag and dumped a number of large denomination crumpled bills on the table, just as

Life Lesson:
The best way to help someone is to fully understand their situation.

Dale, a mortgage broker who was working with us, entered the room to complete a buyer prequalification letter for the offer. Eyeing the pile of bills, he calmly asked what she did for a living.

"Telephone solicitation," she responded, after an awkward pause.

"That's fine," he replied. "How do you get paid?"

"I'm commissioned," she assured him.

"Do you file a tax return?"

"Well, actually, no I don't."

"Let me ask you this, then," Dale continued. "Are you a prostitute?"

At that, our agent jumped to his feet, but before he could speak out to defend his client, she replied "Why yes, I am."

"That's not a problem then," Dale said calmly. "Since you don't declare your income, we'll simply have to do a limited documentation loan at a slightly higher rate."

The Mouse in the Kitchen

Once, after finishing a walk-through of a potential new listing, a beautiful home with lots of character, I sat at the kitchen table with the property owner and consulted my copious notes in order to accurately price the property.

Only then did I realize that I hadn't recorded whether the stove was gas or electric, and when I went to check, I discovered a few holes in the hardwood flooring that appeared to go straight through to the basement. I couldn't understand what they were

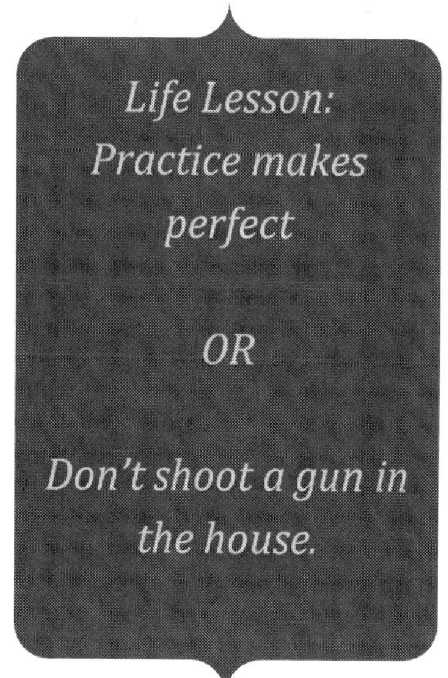

doing in the middle of the floor. Holes often exist in the floors of old homes in order to run wiring, pipes and the like, but these holes were lined up in the middle of the floor, not against a wall.

When I asked what they were doing there, the owner said "Well, my grandfather still has a license to carry a gun. He carries it in a shoulder holster."

"Okay." I said hesitantly.

"Well, we were eating dinner here a few months ago and a mouse ran across the floor. It's a farmhouse, so mice get in sometimes. Anyway, he pulled the gun and opened fire on the mouse."

"Wow, did he get the mouse?"

"No."

Chapter 4:
Understanding Relationships

Relationships are complicated and challenging. They can lead to comfort, joy, and happiness or they can lead to stress, frustration, anxiety and depression. For example, we treat spouses differently than co-workers and siblings differently than our parents or children. Each person and each group of people view us differently depending on their experiences with us and their frame of reference. They may have different expectations of us and we may have different expectations of them.

As I mentioned earlier in this book, selling homes is not as easy as most people believe when they first enter the field of real estate. Most people begin their careers believing that once they pass a license exam, they can sit at the office, waiting for clients to skip in, dropping rose petals in their wake. Worse, they believe it's a simple matter to find the perfect home for clients and make everyone so happy that doves will be released and everyone will sing happily in a park somewhere while holding hands.

Of course, this isn't the case. Furthermore, a realtor's life is complicated by the fact that moving may be a very stressful time in a person's life or a family's life. When people are placed under pressure, they tend to become emotional and frustrated, and may take that frustration out on the person closest to the transaction, in this case – you guessed it – the realtor himself.

As previously mentioned, some of the major stresses that drive customers to sell their homes include a death in the family, the inability of the family to pay the mortgage, a job loss that reduces the family income, a job relocation that forces the family to change locations, and, of course, divorce. Some customers will outright lie to us about their situation because they believe it will impact our estimation of what their home is worth. If they're in foreclosure, they don't want us to know. If they're in the middle of a divorce, they may feel embarrassed.

On the other hand, other customers try to involve us in their problems. In some divorce cases, for example, one of the parties often believes that the realtor is taking sides, which results in attempts to persuade us that they are right. Personally, my only goal is to sell the property, and in the process make it clear that as far as I am concerned, I represent them both.

Understanding Client's on an Emotional Level

Real estate salespeople have great opportunities to attend workshops that will help them to excel in their careers. In the two and a half decades I've been in real estate, I've attended a lot of workshops and, to my delight, have been able to learn from some of the best mentors and trainers in the industry. One of my favorite mentors was a gentleman named Joe Stumpf, a brilliant real estate trainer from California.

I had just returned from a wonderful three day conference during which Joe had told us that, in order to truly assist our clients, we needed to understand their needs to buy and sell on as deep an emotional level as possible. If we could accomplish this, he told us, we would be able to connect with them in a way which would result in subsequent referrals.

For example, our client may be moving across the country because of a job relocation, but it is useful to know precisely what had driven the client to take that step. Perhaps they had no choice in the matter. If so, were they embracing the move as a fresh opportunity, or were they angry and resentful about leaving their friends? This kind of in-depth understanding helps us to really connect with the clients on a much deeper level. We're not just selling a house. We're helping the owners achieve their goals.

> *Life Lesson: Rational people may act completely irrationally under the right conditions or in the right situation.*

The way our instructor taught us to tap into the client's motivation was to respond to each of their statements with the question "Why is that important to you?" Whatever the client said, we would respond by asking "Why is that important to you?" If we had enough guts to ask ten or eleven times in a row, we would, he assured us, get to that deep level of connection and understanding.

However, as I mentioned earlier, some clients lie to us, usually because they are afraid that if we know the true situation, it will impact our evaluation of the likely price range of their home, although of course, this typically is not the case. Some clients, who we later discover are close to bankruptcy, and close to losing their homes, tell us that they're in great financial shape. They really believe that if they give us the incentive of potentially buying another, more expensive house we're more likely to work harder to sell this one. But the truth is, we really need to understand the actual situation in order to help the client to the best of our ability. People may appear to be forthright about the reason for a move.

They may present themselves as a contented couple when actually they are on the brink of a divorce which, for some reason or other, they do not want us to know about.

The evening after my return from the workshop, I had an appointment to give a listing presentation to Mr. and Mrs. D, new clients who had a beautiful brick ranch near a park, not far from my office.   After the customary walk-through, I sat between them at the kitchen table and explained my twenty step home marketing program.

"This is a lovely home, and the location is excellent," I told them. "I bet you take advantage of being so close to the park."

"Yes, we take walks regularly." Mrs. D replied.

"You didn't mention on the phone why you are considering selling," I continued. "Are you considering accepting a job relocation?"

"No," Mr. D explained. "We're planning to move to a larger home."

"Why is a larger home important to you?" I asked, starting my run of eleven questions.

When he fumbled with an answer, I pressed ahead. "How much were you thinking of asking for this property?"

Mr. D gave me a range of values, and I continued to probe. "I understand that you need to get as much money as you possibly can for this home, but I'm curious. Why is this particular price range important to you?"

I continued to pound away with one "Why is that important to you" after another until finally I went a little too far since, as it turned out, my last question took us to the emotional center of the move. "Because she slept with every one of my friends," Mr. D raged. "That's why this move is important to me!"

Suddenly, they were both on their feet, and before I could register what was happening, ran out of the room, he in one direction and she, weeping, in another. It was not the first time I had inadvertently put my foot in my mouth, but it certainly was the topper.

Part of me thought I should pack up my stuff and run for the door. Part of me thought I should go after one or both of them and talk to them, but I was frozen in indecision. Eventually, both of them, calmer, came back to the kitchen table, and we settled on a price.

Interestingly, despite the blow-up my questions cause, I've received more than a dozen referrals from them over the years. However, despite my success getting to the emotion behind the sale, that was the first and last time that I ever asked the question, "Why is that important to you?"

The Indignant Woman

The power of rationalization continues to amaze me. People can convince themselves of nearly anything. The entire concept that there's a hole in the ozone over Antarctica comes to mind, but I'll leave that for later.

For example, I'm certain I've had far more than a hundred occasions in my career in which a wife wanted to sit and explain to me exactly why she felt she had to leave her husband. Either, they feel they have to justify their position or they just want to talk and I happen to be there. In more than half of these conversations, wives have given me variations of the same story, and it's not one I ever hear in the news, so I'd like to share it.

This story is the one in which the husband works long hours and stops paying attention to her and to the family. As a consequence, she becomes involved in other activities and finds someone who truly cares about her, and possibly the kids, with the result that she believes the divorce may even be better for the children. In many cases the wife is very angry with her husband for *driving her into* another man's arms. "How dare he be out working all the time, avoiding time with the family?" they'll say. "I wasn't going to put up with it one more minute."

If I were to be honest, I'd probably ask why these soon-to-be ex-wives really think their husband works so hard, although perhaps I take this situation too personally, because I tend to work more than ten hours each day. I believe many men and women work hard *because* they are trying to provide a good home for the family and are concerned about being able to pay the bills. As successful as I've been, I still worry that I'm only a few months away from losing everything. If I were disabled, for example, there would not be enough money in the bank to cover our expenses for a long period.

At the risk of offending every woman in my reading audience, I also realize that women tend to get part of their identity from their children, their family life and their connections to friends and relatives. This is a generalization, of course, and there are many working women who make being successful in their careers a significant priority, but I believe many, if not most, women tend to assume a family persona, while men, in general, get much of their identity from their work, their accomplishments and their ego. Remember that boys compete fiercely with each other in sports or in school when they're younger, while girls have more of a tendency to connect with their friends on another level. Certainly girls compete and in some cases can be fiercely mean with each other, but they also connect and develop relationships very differently than boys.

On one particular occasion, Andy, a stay-at-home mom in Whitehall, Pennsylvania, talked to me at length about her husband, who she continually referred to as "that bastard" because he worked too much, missed the kid's soccer games, was regularly late for dinner, and didn't volunteer at the school like "every other parent." So she found the perfect guy, who happened to live next door, a man who really cared about her, took the kids to the park during the day and sat and talked for hours. Of course, he was unemployed because his wife was supporting him, but that never really entered our conversation.

When Andy's husband arrived to sign the listing about a half hour into my interview with her, she greeted him with scorn. "You're a bastard," was all she said to him as he entered the room, wearing that horrible deer-in-the-headlights look. Taking a seat across from me, he said weakly, "What do I have to sign?"

Interestingly, I had a meeting with my staff at the office one day and presented them with Andy's story because I was curious as to whether or not anyone shared my opinion of this sort of situation. "Do you think she was right in leaving him, or do you believe she was justifying the fact that she cheated on him with the next door neighbor?"

Uniformly, the men said how terrible this was. The women, with only one exception, argued that the man probably didn't work *all* the time, and that, no doubt, he was having an affair, too, and that she, being intuitive, like most of her sex, had picked up on, and taken her revenge by embarking on her own sexual adventure. "And she would be justified in doing so," one of them told me.

"Wow," I thought. Where in the world did an assumption like that come from? In the end it confirmed my opinion that women tend to defend other women, just as men stick up for men, even though if, somewhere in the process, the truth goes missing.

This year, approximately fifteen couples from my church's congregation screened a movie called *Fireproof* staring Kirk Cameron. Based on the best-seller of the same

> *Life Lesson: Marriage is for better or worse. No marriage or relationship is perfect all the time. Strive to make the best of what you have.*

name and the follow up book called *The Love Dare*, the movie is about a couple having marital difficulties. Although the husband yells at the wife early in the film, he accepts a dare from his father to make himself the best husband he can be in anticipation of being able to put their troubled relationship back together.

Without spoiling the film or novel, both of which I highly recommend you go purchase immediately, the couple remains together, at least through the first half of the film. I won't give away the second half. But at the beginning, while the husband tries to reconnect with her, the wife begins flirting with a male co-worker, meeting him for lunch and gradually becoming emotionally invested in this new individual while married to her husband.

At some point in mid-movie, it is revealed that her co-worker is actually also married, and has been hiding his ring in his desk. What interested me most about the situation was that there was a collective growl from the audience when it was revealed that the co-worker was married. Nice, church-going women in the audience used terms like "slime ball" and "scumbag."

At the end of the film, where I asked my wife and several other women why they were so appalled that the male co-worker had attempted to cheat, they looked at me like I had three heads.

"Are you suggesting it would be okay for him to cheat on his wife? He's just another typical man trying to get laid."

"Why, then, didn't everyone groan when the star's wife began flirting with this co-worker?"

"That's different," they chided me. "She was in a bad marriage. Did you see how he yelled at her? Did you miss the beginning of the movie?"

Was this, I wondered, a double standard? If she had yelled at him for not being home, failing to clean up or forgetting something like their anniversary, would he then have the right to go out and start trying to pick up women? Overall, I think it is a great movie and a great book, but it helps to illustrate how people don't often apply the same standards equally.

Of course, my own feelings and beliefs may be impacted by the fact that I can be very jealous. When once, at church, an older gentleman came up to my wife, took her hand in his and asked a question while continuing to hold her hand, I just about jumped out of my skin. Perhaps it was an overreaction, but I find it very difficult, as no doubt do others, to change the person I am.

The other interesting reason I hear from both men and women to justify their pending divorce is "I'm just not happy and I have the right to be happy, don't I?" I never know how to answer this, except to say that everyone's marriage has ups and downs. After all, we are told in no uncertain terms that marriage is "for better or worse" by the minister, judge, ship's captain or Elvis impersonator.

Life is not perfect, and yes, we'd all love to be happy all the time. But let's consider, though, the implications of divorce on the kids, the family, the pet lizard, not to mention the impact on your finances for the next five to ten years as you try to rebuild your life.

My honest belief is that it has become far too easy to get married and far too easy to get divorced. Please don't misunderstand me. I honestly believe you should do what makes you happy, as long as it's legal, moral, ethical and won't hurt someone else. If you're unhappy in your career and you hate going to work each day, find a way to do something else. The happiest people I've met are those that really enjoy what they do for a living.

Curt Cameron, President of Thomas Hooker Brewery and, as far as I know, no relation to Kirk, once told a group of entrepreneurs that his passion was, "waking up every day and enjoying the passing of time." Hopefully all of us can find a passion rather than a job in our lives.

Problems in the environment that surround each of us can affect the way we interact with those closest to us. We are continually bombarded with challenges, including difficult work schedules, bad bosses, unfair situations, illness, money problems, car accidents, plumbing leaks and many more. Our expectations are seldom in alignment with our real situation or our position in life. We tend to take out our frustrations on those closest to us, which includes our spouses, children, friends and family. All of us need to have a little more patience with each other. We need to work harder to keep marriages and families intact and weather the storms.

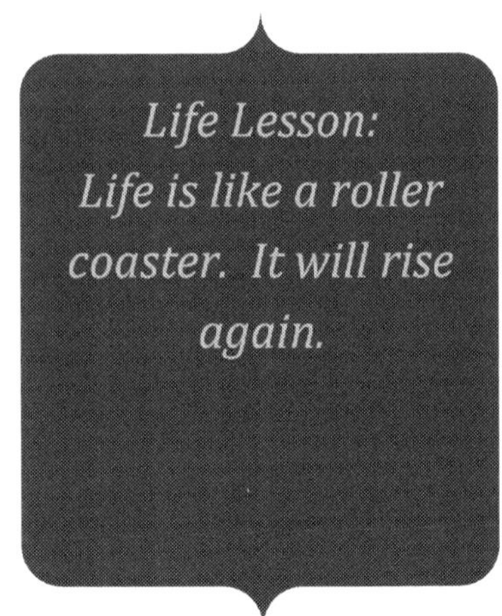

Abuse, of course, is a very rational reason for separating. Physical violence, substance abuse and infidelity are all solid reasons that break up marriages. Several times, over the years, it has been necessary for me to meet with husbands and wives separately because "Protection from Abuse" court orders prevented them from being within a certain distance of each other. In a few cases, the wife was in hiding because the husband had beaten her and she was scared for her life.

Interestingly enough, I rarely hear that a divorce was caused by the husband's infidelity, which seems counter intuitive since the news, movies and books all make it seem that virtually every divorce is due to a cheating husband. On the other hand, perhaps wives are embarrassed, or it simply indicates that I haven't had significant contact with that particular cross section of clients. I will outline, however, some of the more interesting stories of male infidelity later in the chapter.

One other really interesting aspect of male infidelity is that those men who *have* admitted to me that they had been unfaithful have often gone on to explain that they really loved their wives, and that they have, in following their roving eye, made the biggest mistake of their lives. Ah, the lower brain at work!

Speaking of the lower brain, some studies indicate that internet porn has reached an all time high, accounting for more income than Microsoft, Google, Amazon and eBay combined, meaning there may be as many individuals surfing the web to find pornography as there are to make purchases. This is a sad commentary on modern life and the fantasizing brought on by this material is probably part of what leads to acting on those fantasies.

Again, I don't want anyone assuming that I'm taking the side of men in all divorces. I've seen some wickedly controlling men who have done everything possible to hurt their former wives mentally and emotionally and in some cases physically. I've actually been told some tragic stories, both from husbands and wives, involving charges of child abuse, fabricated for the express purpose of hurting their partner. Some have sent private pictures to the former spouse's co-workers, and many other spiteful acts that I probably can't repeat here.

These hurts can run very deep and emotionally scar everyone involved for many years. Don Blose, the managing director of Gideon Promotional Products, one of the country's best real estate promotional products firms, told me that his neighbor is still so bitter about his ex-wife that he kept a lot of her "stuff" and every New Year's Eve, has a "get together" with friends and burns something of hers on the lawn.

The Husband, the Wife and the Girlfriend

On a balmy Monday afternoon, I rang the doorbell of a home I hoped to list in Whitehall. The door was answered by an attractive eastern European woman in her early thirties who introduced herself as the wife and led me to the kitchen table to discuss their situation. We were joined there by her husband, a tall and handsome man with a strong tan and a stronger handshake, and another woman he introduced as his girlfriend.

Although I've had many occasions where one spouse was leaving the other for some third party, I had never actually been seated at a table with all three parties simultaneously. Although I felt distinctly uncomfortable, the other three at the table seemed to be unbothered by the odd situation. Apparently, the husband had begun a relationship with this woman and then moved her into the home to the dismay of his wife.

The husband, refusing to leave the premises, moved down the hall to another bedroom with his girlfriend, while the wife continued to occupy the master bedroom. After nearly a year of a cold war in the home, they mutually decided to sell the property and go their separate ways. And yes, there were children living in home as well.

Since that day, several years ago, I have encountered two more instances in which a home was shared by the man's wife and his mistress. Were I to conduct a relationship with someone outside my marriage, I'm fairly certain my wife would take such umbrage that she might use a sharp implement to cause me bodily harm. I can't quite imagine bringing such infidelity home and moving her in with us.

Hooker Beer

Last week, a very angry client called to complain that their large master bedroom suite was listed in the multiple listing system as "a master bedroom suite." She felt the term was derogatory and insensitive and wanted it removed. I explained that I couldn't remove it because "master bedroom suite" was a term hard-coded into most of the MLS systems that we used and many of the real estate websites.

Ignoring me, she explained that although she was not of any protected class, she wanted to be socially responsible and therefore we'd need to use a different term. "Main bedroom" or "primary bedroom" would be preferable. "I can't remove it," I explained slowly. "The MLS has a checklist of features and we simply check off those features that apply to the home. There is no checkbox for "main bedroom" or "primary bedroom." She hung up on me.

Slightly off the subject, but related, when I mentioned Curt Cameron earlier in this chapter, I recalled that I was at a workshop this year with the president of the Thomas Hooker Brewing Company, which makes Thomas Hooker beer, a variety of micro-brews from Connecticut. Thomas Hooker was the founder of Hartford, Connecticut and a Puritan minister, which latter fact may explain why, unlike other brews, Hooker Beer does not feature scantily clothed women in their advertising.

Nevertheless, lots of people have fun with the name Hooker Beer, which has led to some outrageous and arguably hysterical T-shirts, an example being, "No wife, no girlfriend, no date, grab a Hooker." Another is "Hooker Beer… always a happy ending".

The president of the company said that once he had taken over, he received a call from a woman he knew who proceeded to plow into him about the name and its general degradation of women. "How dare you continue the name of this brewery. Women are never prostitutes because they want to be. They are forced into prostitution by this male dominated society and their deep need for financial independence in this world of men who control the purse strings." Wow!

Recently, I read about twenty three year old Natalie Dylan of San Diego, California who had graduated from college with a degree in Women's Studies, and in order to pay for graduate school, auctioned off her virginity for nearly four million dollars, a story that, quite naturally, made headlines.[ii]

Now, let's be honest. Did she need four million dollars? Aren't there guaranteed student loans for practically everybody? I realize that many women are forced into an ugly and despicable lifestyle that in many ways is akin to slavery, and I'm certain we could argue this subject back and forth for hours. There are no easy answers, but honestly, lighten up. Hooker Beer is a bottle of liquid named after the town's Christian founder.

Some people try too hard to find something that offends them.

Wooing my Bride

For many years, two of my best friends were Deb and Harry Hartman. At the graduation party of their twin daughters, I met a young woman named Theresa who was lovely in every way. I liked the way she looked, the way she stood and during a long and interesting conversation with her, she mentioned that she was an office manager at a local personnel company and that she was taking real estate classes which meant that we had something in common.

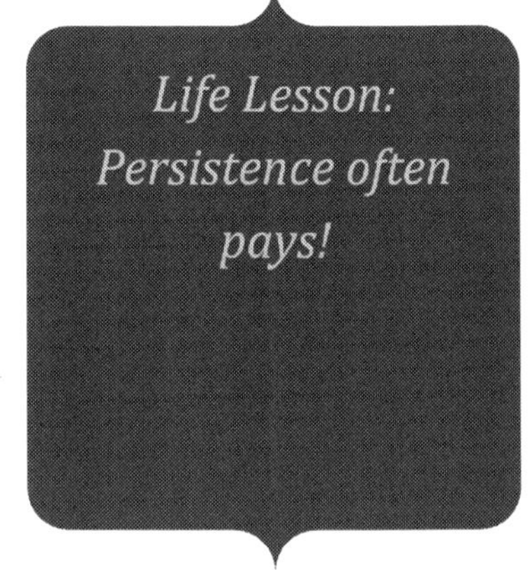

At the end of the evening, I asked if she'd like to go out some time, eliciting the response that, although she was certain I would make a pleasant companion, she had recently broken off a relationship and wasn't looking for another one. She wanted some time to herself. I gracefully acknowledged the blow-off and pretended not to be hurt, but I couldn't stop thinking about her.

The next day, I sent flowers to Theresa at the personnel company. She called and thanked me, but she said she really wasn't interested. I seemed like a nice guy, but the answer was still 'No.'

The following day, I once again sent her flowers. She called immediately and told me that she thought she had made her feelings plain. She was not interested. She would not go out with me and I should please stop bothering her. She finished the announcement by firmly saying "No *really* means no. It does not mean I'm playing hard to get."

On the third day, my thick headed Irish side took over and I again sent her flowers. "I just want you to understand," she began on her call to me, "that I consider this stalking and possibly harassment. If it doesn't end, I may have to take action against you."

"Listen," I replied. "I won't send you flowers again. I promise. However, you told me that you are taking real estate classes. I don't know who you're planning to affiliate with, but whoever it is, it's a mistake, because my firm offers better training, better marketing, the best commission structure available and we even offer profit sharing. Is it possible for us to get together *just* to talk about your career path and what my firm can offer you? I promise not to ask you anything personal."

"That sounds fine," she said.

"Great, why don't we do it over dinner? I'll pick you up at six."

I immediately drove over to Deb Hartman's office, reasoning that, since she had also been a guest at Deb's party, she might be able to fill me in on Theresa's background. I was, you see, determined not to take any false steps.

However, she couldn't remember a Theresa being at the party. Most of the guests had been friends and acquaintances of the Hartman's from their work in title insurance. But after I had described Theresa, a light apparently went off in Deb's head and she grabbed my arm and warned me not to date her because she was her goddaughter. I gathered that, despite the fact that we both knew that Theresa was twenty-five, Deb still thought of her as a child.

A year and a half later, we were married despite the great challenges of dating!

Crazy Divorces

Divorce negatively impacts all members of the family. It does, however, allow divorce attorneys to purchase large homes and fancy cars.

I was sitting with a couple who had bought and sold several homes with me over a fifteen year period. Michael vacillated between being extremely angry and, apparently, hurt, so much so that, several times, he was on the verge of tears. Rebecca was flat and to the point. She had lost weight and looked much better than I had seen her years earlier.

"Michael, I'm not happy," she said. "We are *not* staying together, and we need to sign the listing to sell this house."

"You can't stop me from trying," he replied. "I don't want to see our family split up. What if you change your mind? I'm still willing to take you back, and if we sell the home and you do that, we'd be starting completely over. Why don't we take a few more days and cool down. I mean, the only way I wouldn't take you back is if you were to have sex with another man."

"Well then, Michael, I'll let you know that that ship has sailed."

I tried looking in any direction except at the couple. My father raised me to avoid showing emotion. Men are supposed to be strong and not put their weaknesses on display. This fact might explain why I'm not very good with overly emotional clients. I want to solve their problems, but I simply don't know how to react. As a result, I know I sometimes appear cold or unfeeling because, instead of dealing with a problem emotionally, I tend to problem solve.

In some divorce situations, the husband and wife can't agree on selling the property. One of them would like keep the house, but can't afford to pay the mortgage or buy the other party out. If one moves out and both fail to pay the mortgage, both of their credit scores will be destroyed, making it nearly impossible to get a new mortgage for either of them.

In several cases, either the husband or wife fails to pay the mortgage intentionally, because they actually want the property to go to foreclosure simply to ruin the

> *Life Lesson: People will wrestle with right and wrong and ultimately defend whatever position they take.*

other's credit. Initially, both may sign a listing contract, and we may receive an offer, but the angry party refuses to sign the sales contract in order to keep the property marching toward foreclosure.

In some of these cases we've tried to assist clients by getting them and their attorney into court to file a motion claiming the spouse is a hostile seller, that there is no reason for the spouse to refuse to sign off on selling the property other than to hurt their partner. In most cases, the Court has agreed, and forced the sale of the property.

In one case, however, when we placed the property on the market for sale, and put up our Century 21 gold post, the home owner, the husband, came out of the house with an axe, and chopped it in half down the middle to let us know exactly what he thought of selling the property.

At the time we used wooden posts, today we use aluminum or PVC.

In another situation, a wife was upset because her husband, Jacob, worked such long hours, and in order to show him just how upset she was, she entered into an affair with an employee whose desk faced her husband's. She then told her Jacob about the affair, hoping to torture her husband as daily he faced the man who slept with his wife.

We listed the home a few weeks later.

Chapter 5:
Sometimes Stuff Just Happens

As I mentioned earlier in the book, my first experience of selling a home was embarrassing for both me and the home sellers. Regrettably, it's not the only time that has happened. Worse, I find myself in some sort of embarrassing situation that involves nudity or humiliation about once every other year, situations which, although never my fault, usually result in my being screamed at or chewed out.

In one instance, we had a two-unit apartment building under agreement in west Allentown. And since the agreement of sale was contingent on a building inspection, we informed the tenants that a building inspector would be coming to the property at a specific time the next day. The building inspector was early.

Instead of knocking, he simply used the lockbox and walked into the first floor apartment, which was occupied by a young, single Latino woman who spoke very little English. As luck would have it, this being a one level apartment, she stepped out of the bathroom, wrapped in a towel, just in time to collide with the inspector who, despite her screams, insisted that he had every right to be here.

The police were called. The landlord was called. And I was called. The tenant was extremely upset that this unapologetic and overbearing gentleman - and I use this term loosely - had seen her naked and had refused to leave, regardless of whether or not he had an appointment. In this case, I fully expected to be involved in a lawsuit, but, thankfully, that didn't happen.

The next year, we had a similar situation. The Chief Operating Officer (COO) of a moderate sized insurance company had married a young woman who had all the qualities and look of any fashion model. They had a beautiful Mediterranean-style home with an in-ground pool and some great areas to entertain. We were called in to market the home because the couple was divorcing. The husband had already left and moved out of the area. The wife was more than a little unhappy about selling the home and moving to something smaller.

She, although polite enough, was certainly not the warm and fuzzy type. But, as several of the other agents pointed out, she was extremely attractive which was, perhaps the reason I found her a little intimidating.

On a Monday morning, she stormed our office to speak with our office manager, Tim, and me about what she referred to as a gross invasion of her privacy. Evidently a realtor had shown up early the prior morning, without our office confirming an appointment. She heard the rattling of the front door and raced down the steps to find the agent, from a competing firm, standing in her foyer. Being dressed in only a short tank-top and a pair of lacy underwear, she shouted at him to leave immediately and he refused, stating that he had an appointment. An argument ensued, after which she ran upstairs to change.

She had, as a consequence, come in the office to express that she had been visually violated and wanted action taken against the realtor in question. I wasn't sure there was much we could do, since he worked for another firm, but I assured

Life Lesson:
Learn to forgive.

her we'd do our best. My intent was to contact the Board of Realtors to determine if, when a realtor enters a home without permission, a law has been broken.

The reason the story stuck in my mind was the way this home owner had described the situation, graphically indicating each part of her body which the agent must have seen, with the result that Tim and I were trying to concentrate on the legal ramifications of this situation while she was giving us the equivalent of an erotic phone call.

However, alls well that ends well. After the house went under contract, her husband thanked us profusely for our hard work.

Unfortunately, his wife was not as kind.

Hanging from a Cliff

There have been several occasions in my career when my car has become stuck in mud, snow or ice, requiring me to summon help to dislodge it. Although these situations occur less frequently now that I've begun purchasing large gas-guzzling, environmentally unfriendly SUV's with 4-wheel-drive rather than Cadillac's or sports cars, they have caused me quite a bit of embarrassment over the years.   Several of our agents in the firm have had similar experiences.

One of the reasons for this problem is that, although my firm and I sell virtually every type of real estate from mobile homes and urban row homes to luxury estates to office buildings, one of our primary specialties is the farmette, a property with enough acreage so that the owner could, if he liked, have a barn and some animals, perhaps horses.

On fifty plus acre properties, we'll often find gravel drive-ways or areas that haven't been properly plowed. On larger properties, buyers may want to drive the entire property rather than walk it, and I'm here to assure you that tall wet grass can also cause problems for traction.

On one occasion, Joe Bartera was finalizing a sale at a beautiful French Chateau north of the Poconos, having sold the million dollar estate to a best-selling author as a weekend retreat. By the time Joe had finished with all the paperwork, he found that his small sports car wouldn't make it back up the long five hundred foot driveway, which was now covered with snow and ice. A quick call to AAA informed him that they would not tow the car that far off the road on private property. As a result, I made the hour and a half journey from my home to the property to assist him, and arrived just as he was finally pulling out of the driveway, having taken him that long to travel the five hundred feet from the home to the road.

On another occasion several years ago, I received a frantic call from one of our female agents who had become stuck in a muddy driveway. And since someone had to push the car and her client was elderly, she had been the one to do it, in the course of which her skirt had split down the back. She was, she told me, hiding out in the bathroom until someone from the office could bring her something else to wear.

My worst experience occurred about fifteen years ago, northwest of Allentown, when I was working with an older couple that was relocating into the area and wanted something secluded in a wooded setting. It was probably mid-January and only a day after an ice storm when we went out house hunting. It was still bitter cold.

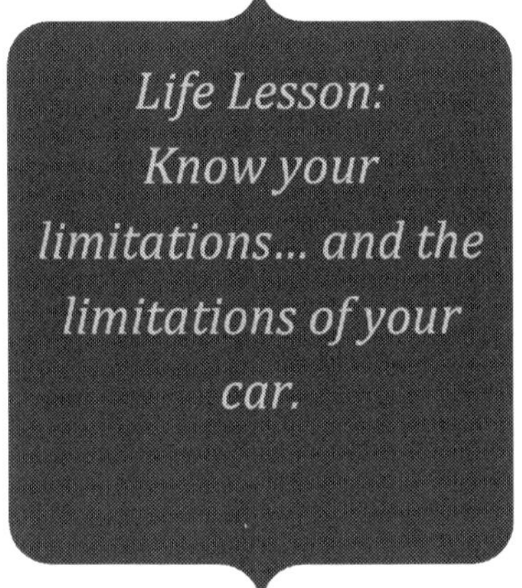

Although the major roads were in good shape, the streets in this rural area had not been properly cleaned and salted. Still, we managed to get through the first two properties without incident. The final house was situated at the top of the mountain, and I carefully wound my Plymouth around the curves in the road, moving steadily toward the peak. With road conditions worsening, I assured the buyers that my car was equipped with all weather tires and that there would not be a problem.

However, just short of the property, with a sheer drop on the passenger side of the car, we began to slide. Panicking, I overcompensated and sent us into a spin toward the ravine. One breathtaking moment later, the car came to rest against a tree, with the front third of the car hanging out over the steep drop.

The older couple carefully climbed out of the back of the car, and I followed. My cell phone had no signal and the home they were to view, being vacant, had no phone service. In the bitter cold, we hiked back down the winding icy road looking for a house from which we could summon help. However, all the houses we passed were apparently weekend retreats, closed for winter, which meant that it took us close to an hour to get to a telephone.

Ultimately, it took a truck with a small crane to extricate my car from its precarious position. It came as no surprise to me when the elderly couple elected to choose another agent to assist them with finding their dream home.

Horses?

Michelle received a call from a gentleman from New York who had a very strong Brooklyn accent. Since my team is well known for selling farmettes, the gentleman decided we'd be the best source to find him a large parcel that was fertile and most importantly, very private. Money was no object.

Boots and jeans tend to be the outfit of choice for most buyers looking at large farms because, in all likelihood, they will leave with some dirt and grime on them. The large gentleman who met Michelle that weekend was wearing a suit, a long coat and very nicely shined black leather shoes.

Also unusual was the fact that he was not accompanied by a wife or girlfriend, but rather by two other large gentlemen dressed in the same fashion.

Michelle walked the second property with them, talking the entire time. They crested a hill and descended into a valley that had complete privacy.

"This is perfect," the buyer said to his friends. "No one can see nothing here."

"That's great," Michelle replied, ignoring the double negative. "How many horses do you have?"

They all turned to stare at her. "Horses?" He replied. "What horses? I don't have any $@&!#$ horses."

Michelle figured she'd never make it back to the office.

Rock Stars

My firm services the region of Eastern Pennsylvania between Philadelphia and the Pocono Mountains including the Lehigh Valley, Bucks County and the Poconos. The Lehigh Valley, or Allentown-Bethlehem area, is located about an hour and twenty minutes west of New York City and less than an hour north of Philadelphia. The convenient location and rural feel make it the perfect place for many of our more successful New York clients to get away from the city to enjoy a completely different lifestyle.

Some of our clients have included actors, rock stars, politicians, sports figures, best-selling authors and other celebrities, people with whom we are often required to sign a confidentiality agreement in order to avoid the possibility of fans or paparazzi ruining the peace and quiet of their Pennsylvania retreat. In some cases, for the same reason, the properties are bought in the name of a straw party. At other times, the celebrities don't really care whether we talk about them or not.

On one occasion, a young man came to see me about buying a secluded horse farm with a mountain view. He added that he preferred not to deal with anyone except me, an odd request, but one which I promptly assured him would be the case, after which, pushing down his dark glasses, he said, "No need for introductions then. I know who you are and you most certainly have recognized me."

Actually, I was drawing a blank, although I did not want to say so. Was he, I wondered, a rock star, one of those celebrities who someone like myself, who is fond of music from the 80s and 90s, would scarcely know.

> *Life Lesson: Everyone wants attention. The best way to a person's heart is to give them that attention.*

"I don't want any of my fans knowing I'm here," he told me. "I need to have you give me some sort of confidentiality paperwork."

"Sure, that's no problem." I retrieved the forms, all the while racking my brain to determine if I had ever heard the name before and since nothing came to me, I asked for his last name in order to fill in the form.

He stared at me as though I were an alien from outer space. "Don't you know who I am?" he demanded.

"Uh, no, I'm really sorry, but I honestly have no idea who you are," I told him meekly, always master of witty repartee.

"I've sold millions of CDs!" He cried.

Having gone this far in exposing my ignorance, I decided to go a step further.

"What kind of music do you play?" I asked, at which point he apparently gave up the effort to impress me completely, after which, surprisingly enough, we got on very well.

Many of the celebrities or wealthy clients we've worked with have been very down-to-earth people. Frank Langella, for example, while looking at homes with me, introduced me to antique quilt collecting. And since I have 1940's super hero action figures on my desk, and I regularly wear cartoon ties, no collectible seems odd to me. Frank, despite being a burley actor who specializes in powerful roles turned out to love antique quilts. And since Pennsylvania is a treasure trove of them, our house hunting trips frequently turned into shopping tours which, to my surprise, I enjoyed as much as he.

All which proves, in this business, you never know.

Another well known individual from the artistic community, who shall remain nameless, looked at a very secluded farm an hour and a half outside New York, the kind of place that he planned to make into a weekend retreat. And because this property appeared to be perfect for him, he asked if we could leave him in the middle of the pasture behind the home so that he could, as he put it, meditate and commune with the natural surroundings. That was certainly a first. We left him alone for forty-five minutes. Apparently his communing went well, because he purchased the property and moved in the following month.

Pet Problems

Pets can cause realtors all sorts of pain. Dog and cat lovers may not recognize the pet odors in the home because they live with them. As a consequence, it is often a real challenge to be forced to explain that unless they find a way to eliminate the smell, no one will buy their house, a typical response being, "What smell? My home doesn't smell!"

Other home sellers tell us that we can show the home absolutely any time, even though their pet pit bull is in the living room when the owners aren't home. After all, Muffin the pit bull wouldn't hurt a fly. What pet lovers often fail to understand is that many buyers are reluctant to enter a home where Muffin is not on a leash tied with iron to a very strong wall.

A number of years ago, one of our agents had scheduled a showing for a nice suburban home. The owners asked him to use the lockbox and enter through the laundry room door, neglecting however to tell him that she had guard dogs and more importantly, forgot to lock them up.

The following day, when he and his client stepped into the laundry room, shutting the exterior door behind them, two large dogs, growling and snapping, charged into the small room with them, causing Marvin to leap backward through an open door which led into a half bath. Slamming it shut, he left the buyer scaling the washing machine, from which vantage point, he banged on the bathroom door and demanded to be let in.

As you might assume, this is one sale that never happened.

Real Estate... A Risky Business

In addition to icy roads and guard dogs, realtors often face a number of other potentially dangerous situations, including one which involved a pet alligator which, the owners being away, had managed to find a way out of his cage.

On another occasion, in the middle of winter, my father, who was selling real estate part time with us, showed a large brick warehouse. The electric was off, and there was little light filtering through the dirty windows at the top of the building. Descending to the lower level of building, he and the buyers noticed that the ceiling appeared very low for warehouse space, and that the floor appeared to be a slick wet transparent tile of some sort, beneath which they could just barely make out a room filled with desks, chairs and filing cabinets. Only then did they realize that the lower level had flooded and frozen, and that they were standing six to eight feet off the floor on a sheet of ice. Needless to say, they made it out of the building quickly but very, very carefully.

That same year, on the afternoon before Christmas Eve, my father showed a vacant home in the slate belt of Pennsylvania which was full of mold and mildew. He and his two clients, who were considering buying the house as an investment, went down to the basement to check the heating system and look over the wiring, in the process of which the basement door slammed shut behind them and latched, locking them in the dark, with no way out. A significant amount of time later, during which they kicked and pounded on the door, they were finally released. But my father never forgot how close he'd come to spending a Christmas locked in a moldy basement with clients.

And, needless to say, he never let me forget, either.

The Torture Chamber Below

And speaking of basements, about twenty years ago, I toured the most unusual basement of my career. A representative of a government agency, having asked our firm to list a property for sale in our market area, gave me keys to the property and told me that the dwelling was a combination home and medical office. The agency wanted me to determine a likely sales price. They did not disclose how it happened that they owned the property.

The home was a large two-story structure in a suburban residential neighborhood only a block or so from an elementary school and playground, the first floor of which constituted a physician's offices including a waiting room, patient rooms and a file storage room. A separate entrance led to the second floor apartment, which was where, I assumed, the doctor had lived.

The truly interesting part of the property was the basement. Just as is true with many homes, the basement had a concrete floor and cinderblock walls but unlike any other basement I had been in, this one was divided into a series of unfinished rooms, each with a heavy steel door and barred window, rather like a jail. Furthermore, there was a drain in the middle of each floor, and at the end of the hallway an incinerator.

I regret to say that I never discovered what use all this had been put to by the doctor or government agency, although several members of my staff came up with wild theories, none of which, unfortunately, served to enhance the value of this particular property.

Dive Bombing Cockroaches

Recently, I was watching my kids play what I assumed was the old "rock, paper, scissors" game until I realized the hand movements did not seem to represent rocks, paper or scissors. And when I asked about it, my son chirped up and said, "We're playing 'foot, cockroach and nuclear explosion."

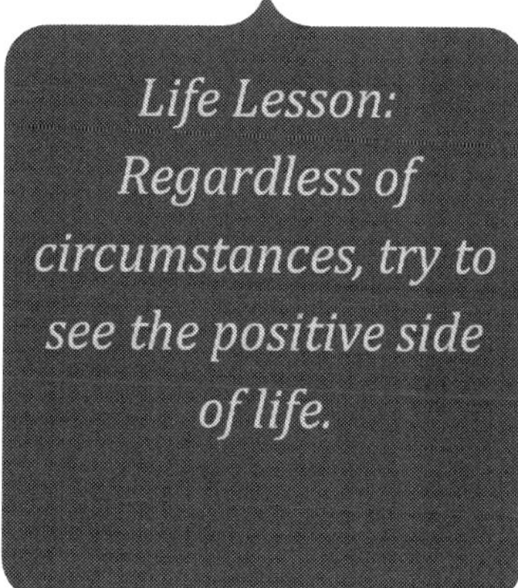

"Foot, cockroach and nuclear explosion?" I asked.

"Foot stomps on cockroach. Cockroach survives a nuclear explosion and nuclear explosion fries the foot."

I am always amazed at how creative kids are, but seriously, what are we teaching them?

One of my favorite gross stories involved cockroaches and a successful agent named Ellie who was the top agent in the firm for many years, selling nearly every type of real estate during her career. On a hot and muggy summer day, Ellie and I met the owner of several apartment buildings at one of his center city multi-units, a filthy property, but one which had been extraordinarily profitable over the years.

Ellie, who always dressed in the most professional way, and took great pains with hair and makeup, could not hide the fact that the condition of the building appalled her.

The landlord stepped into the second apartment, and we followed into the dark room. He crossed to the far wall and turned on the lights. The front room was the kitchen and a wave of cockroaches seemed to swarm the walls from every direction. And when, in the second apartment, a wave of cockroaches greeted us as the landlord turned on the light, some dropping on us from the ceiling, she obviously barely kept from screaming.

I'm afraid that Ellie will never forgive me for that listing appointment!

Don't Let the Cat Out

Last year, I represented a gorgeous horse farm in central Bucks County, one of the priciest areas in the United States. The owner had twenty-two horses on the property, each with their own stall in a barn behind the home. She also had a private indoor riding arena for training purposes.

An agent from a competing firm showed the property to some clients without my being present. Generally, if the property is large or unique, I'll try to accompany showings, but it is not always possible to match the schedules of the buyers, their agent and me.

This particular agent took the clients into the fenced pastures where the horses were grazing.

Unless a buyer or realtor is very familiar with the animals, I never recommend they do this sort of thing since, if someone is injured during a showing, we are apt to be liable. In this case, these buyers and their agent walked the perimeter of the pastures from the inside and left to consider it as a possible purchase.

Subsequently, the owner, who was working on a project in Philadelphia at the time, called me in a panic to say that her neighbor had just phoned her with the news that the showing agent had left the gates open to the pastures and that there were twenty-two horses running around central Bucks County, not far from major roads. She was on her way, but wanted us to get there and help round up the horses before they were hit. Thankfully, all the horses were found and returned.

Life Lesson: Life is unpredictable. Prepare for the worst and expect the best.

A more common situation for realtors is opening the door to a home and having a cat or dog rush past us into the yard. In one instance, another agent shared with me, the owner lectured her in advance to make sure the cat didn't get past her. "The cat usually hides," the owner said, "but just in case, don't let her out." The agent readily agreed.

When the agent arrived at the home, and found a note on the door once again stating that the cat must not be left out of the home, she carefully let her clients into the house, shutting the door behind her. When they were ready to leave, however, she opened the front door to find the cat sitting on the stoop in front. Heart racing, she grabbed the animal and tossed it back in the house, thinking that she had a close call.

A few hours later, the client called her, truly enraged. The cat that the realtor had tossed into the house was a male, belonging to one of the neighbors. And since her cat was female and in heat, this was the last thing she wanted to happen. As my Life Lesson says, life is unpredictable.

Jeff and the Gopher

A local lawn care and landscaping service, Superior Landscaping, is owned by a young man named Jeff Sell, who, among other things, cuts the lawns of those properties our firm handles for relocating clients and bank foreclosures. Jeff is great to work with and the clients love him. If the lawn isn't perfect, he goes over it again and again until it looks great, without an additional charge.

However, we used to think there was a black cloud following Jeff. It started when he was accidentally shot in the chest a few years ago, just after he was married, when an old man with fading eyesight mistook Jeff for a turkey. After recovering from his ordeal, he had a few other crazy experiences that "could only happen to Jeff."

One of them happened during the summer of 2009 when he was with our mortgage broker, Bob Wilfinger at the construction site for a new Pennsylvania Lincoln Log Home. Bob was adding some plantings for us, and Jeff, who was preparing to mow the lawn, informed Bob that during a prior job he had accidentally run over a rabbit. He often hit snakes that hid in the grass, he said, but rabbits would usually run out of the way. This one played possum until it was too late. He said the yard clean-up was horrendous.

With that, Jeff jumped onto his large tractor and proceeded across the field next to the house, cutting a swath in the high grass as he went. And when a gopher popped up, straight in his path, it was too late for Jeff to turn, with the result that the gopher leaped onto the deck of the tractor and jumping onto Jeff's shirt, proceeded to scramble onto his face.

Bob said you could hear Jeff scream from quite a distance!

The Groundhog under the Deck

In another situation, a client and longtime friend of ours had moved into her new home, only to discover a groundhog living under her deck. Making a call to a local hardware store, she asked what types of traps were available to get rid of the pesky rodents, to which an employee of the hardware store explained that one method of repelling them would be to cover the area with lime.

She went out to the local grocery store and purchased an entire box of limes. She had most of them cut into thin slices by the time her husband arrived home and explained that 'lime' was a white powder sold in hardware stores.

Watch the Baby

There are times when we judge ourselves too harshly as well. When a good friend and associate of mine was a new mother, much of her world revolved around her kids.

When her son was a few months old, she carried him into her bedroom to get a diaper and change him. And because he had never even rolled over yet, she left him for a second on the bed in order to reach for a diaper, only to hear a thump that made a chill run up her spine. Sure enough, he had learned to shift positions at the most inopportune time, and had landed on the floor.

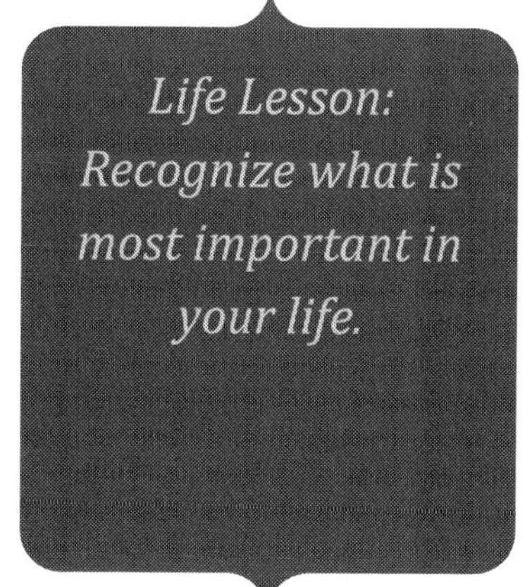

In the two or three seconds that it took her to turn and scoop up her child, she was terrified. What if he had become paralyzed or otherwise seriously injured by the fall? She lifted him, checking every part to look for blood, broken bones or obvious injury. Luckily, he was absolutely fine.

Shaken, she set him back on the bed. This time she sat against him so he couldn't roll off again. She faced the wall and put her head in her hands. If he had been hurt, it would have been her fault, she surmised. She never should have set him on the bed like that.

That's when she heard the second "thud" when he rolled off the other side.

A Dozen Long Stemmed Roses... without the Roses

When I was in high school, my English teacher, Miss S, who had an extremely liberal outlook, told us that she had been furious with her husband when he had allowed himself to be drafted and sent to Vietnam instead of being a "real man," and going to Canada. When he returned, she met him at the airplane, with divorce papers in hand, and condemned him for, as she put it, murdering children.

Although she was a very bright person, she was also highly condescending. At one point, Miss S asked a student to explain a story from the bible, which in my opinion, had very little to do with the subject we were discussing. The girl explained that, not being Christian, she wasn't familiar with the story whereupon she was berated for not being familiar with the parables of the Christian society in which she lived.

At the end of the term, I sent Miss S a dozen long stems, not the roses, just the long stems, along with an unsigned card. However, I addressed it, and of course, she recognized my handwriting.

Miss S wasted no time in calling me into her classroom to tell me that I was a "little boy who would never grow up" and would doubtless never amount to anything, which is seldom a good thing to tell a teenager. I told her that I hoped I'd never grow up. I liked the happy person I was, rather than being someone miserable who looked for reasons to be offended at everyone around me. I didn't add that I was referring to someone like her, but I was sure, from her expression, that she got the point.

> *Life Lesson:*
> *Accept responsibility for your actions. You won't move forward to new challenges until you've acknowledged the mistakes of your past.*

Chapter 6:
Real Estate Agents are as crazy as their clients

Realtors

People are attracted to the real estate sales industry for many different reasons. Two of the primary ones, however, are the flexible hours and limitless income potential. As a broker and manager of real estate salespeople, one of my greatest challenges is that, as I explained in an earlier chapter, many of these new agents also believe their new careers will be relatively easy. After all, everyone wants to own a home, right?

All a new agent has to do is sit by the phone, waiting for that next young couple to come in and purchase a two hundred and fifty thousand dollar townhome, netting him or her a cool five to seven thousand dollars. Unfortunately, a career in real estate sales doesn't work that way.

Oddly enough, flexible hours tend to work against most new realtors. Since each realtor is an independent contractor, he or she can set their own hours, but they need also to set their own agendas. If an agent isn't scheduled to be at the office answering the phone, they tend not to be working. In order to be a success, the realtor has to work hard, proactively prospecting for potential home buyers and sellers.

And, despite the fact that technically the industry does also allow for a virtually limitless income and there are agents across the country earning multi-million dollar incomes each year, a new agent needs to go out and find property sellers and buyers, a process called prospecting.

At risk of being overly repetitive, buying or selling a home can be one of the most stressful times in a person's life. To complicate matters, many of the transactions we handle are based on a client's divorce, job relocation, death in the family or loss of income forcing a sale. These clients may be under a lot of pressure or stress. Some are likely to be volatile in the way they react to bad news, and they tend to blame the person closest to them in the transaction – the realtor.

Realtors, incidentally, have one of the highest rates of divorce and suicide of any profession. You will find, within the ranks of the highly successful Realtors, some of the most religious, ethical and caring individuals in the world, but you will also discover some of the most hardcore alcoholics, drug abusers, and purveyors of infidelity in the ranks of any profession.

The Realtor's Life Cycle

Many of the new real estate salespeople our firm hires seem to follow a similar pattern when they first enter the field. I liken this pattern or career track to a person's life cycle: childhood, teenage years and adulthood. When the new salesperson first begins his or her career, he or she believes everything the manager or broker says. Each agent does most of what is asked, as long as the manager or broker follows up to make sure it's done. I call this the childhood stage of their real estate career. They don't yet fly on their own, but they listen to us as if we're the parent and they believe what we tell them.

Unfortunately, the first stage is followed by something similar to the teenage years. Once the agent has a little success, he or she begins to believe that they know absolutely everything about everything. They stop walking around the office and begin swaggering. They tend to want to change the rules in the office, because the way management does things is obviously outdated. They listen more to other agents than to their manager or broker, much like teenagers primarily listen to other teenagers.

Life Lesson: The happiest people are those who find their passion and then live their passion. Find yours.

Worse, this is the point at which most agents, if they are going to leave a company, leave. Since the agent has had a little success, they stop working as hard, and then, when their sales start slipping, they blame the broker or the company. It must be the broker's poor advertising program, or perhaps the carpet isn't clean enough to appeal to really good clients. Convinced that the grass must be greener somewhere else, they hurry to join another brokerage house.

The bright side is that this teenage stage generally only lasts six months to two years, so if we can get them past those teenage months without beating them to death with a blunt instrument, like perhaps a toaster, stapler or coffee mug, they will become productive adults, consistently delivering good service to their clients and making a stable, steady income.

This brings me to an interesting point about human nature. When everything is not going perfectly, people seem to assign blame to someone else. As I wrote earlier, if a marriage falters, it's always the other party's fault. Even if you cheat on your spouse, it was your spouse that drove you to it. If a salesperson is not doing well, they tend not to look at the market in general, or their own lack of prospecting, preferring to lay the blame at the doorstep of the person doing the marketing and advertising.

If an appliance manufacturer has layoffs, the workers blame the president of the company. It must be his or her poor management, or it must be that two million dollar bonus the management received last year. It can't possibly be the fact that a competitor is now making a better product or the fact that the workers at the factory are earning fifty dollars an hour for assembly line work when workers in China are doing the same job for an hourly wage of thirty-seven cents. It can't be that the retirement pension plan is out of control, and it certainly can't be the fact that property and school taxes on the company's plant have gone up eight hundred percent in the past few years while other countries are subsidizing their companies in order to keep jobs. It all simply falls back on the boss. It's his fault. In the United States, if the economy falters, it must be because of something the President has or hasn't done.

During the twenty-five years I've been in business, I've experienced three real estate recessions. During the first, I was almost forced into bankruptcy when agents began marching into my office, one after another, to tell me that the phone had stopped ringing and they were going to the greener pastures offered by my competitors. When I pointed out that the entire market and every other company's sales were way down, they would cry, "I've heard that XYZ real estate has plenty of buyers! Their phones are ringing!

The broker at XYZ told me so!" Most of these agents who left eventually also left the industry, although some continued to bounce from firm to firm for many years looking for that one great office where the phones ring continually despite the economic situation.

Incidentally, a good real estate agent can make money regardless of market conditions since even in the worst economic recession, there are still properties being bought and sold. There are always tenants renting apartments who want to own their own homes, as well as buyers relocating for jobs, divorcing couples needing to dispose of their homes and deaths requiring the sale of real estate. It simply means that, during downturns, realtors need to engage in more active prospecting.

During the most recent economic crisis, I lost far fewer people and fared much better than many others because I continually warned my agents that this good market would not last forever. I also made a point of sharing ongoing statistics with the staff to show them what was happening across the industry, not just in their particular office, and pointed out what each realtor needed to do in order to survive.

We weren't completely successful in keeping agents, however. One such agent who left during the most recent downturn stands out in my mind as an example of how much our course in life is directed by emotion rather than any logic. "I'm sorry. I love it here, but I have to leave," she said.

"I know your sales are down," I replied, "but so are everyone's. When there are fewer buyers, you need to be more proactive."

"Don't you understand, Loren?" she insisted. "I'm going to lose my house!"

"I *do* understand," I assured her. "What I don't understand is how moving on to a competitor's office will actually help you keep your house. You've built a solid business of referrals here. You would be starting over. Your clients wouldn't immediately know that you made a change, and even when you send them a letter, they may not open it, or they may continue to think of you as working for Century 21 Keim. You could actually be harming your career."

"Loren, when things are bad, you have to change. I hate to do it, but I need to change."

"What you need to change is yourself. You've not been in the office as much. You haven't been sending out your client mailings or newsletters and you're not following up as aggressively as you once did."

"No, when things are bad, you start fresh. You change. That's what I need. I need to change. That will fix everything."

She went to a competing firm and other than having a great sale that originated while she was still with us, she has actually done far worse. Change doesn't fix everything. Everyone goes through rough spots in their lives. Whether we're talking about someone's career or divorce when the marriage is no longer perfect, we have to take the time to look at every situation logically and not be overruled by emotion.

During the most recent presidential election, our company was divided by political party. The conservative minded agents in our firm frequently engaged in heated arguments with their more liberal colleagues. As for me, although I was not excited by John McCain, I was more afraid of Barrack Obama, my reason being that I believed he wanted to socialize more of our institutions, taking more power or control for the central government in the name of helping people. Those who study history realize that centralized control of everything doesn't work. It's simply putting more power into the hands of a select few individuals instead of having that power spread out. Another method of taking control by a central authority is by confiscating individual wealth, effectively keeping everyone at a low level beneath the government.

Also, taking the earnings of those who work hard and giving it to others, in the name of fairness, is a disincentive to anyone who is actually working.

Anyway, as I asked different agents what they liked or didn't like about particular candidates, the number one reason many of our agents liked Barrack was that he stood for change. So my question, naturally, was, "What change are you hoping for?" The answers were usually "a better economy" or "better health care."

But since Obama is an attorney with no background in finance, medicine, or business, it was not clear to me how he would do all that. And when I posed the question, no one ever had an answer. It was an emotional matter for those who saw the economy faltering, one which many felt could be addressed by exchanging one president for another, as though the government could simply wave a magic wand and solve all our problems. Unfortunately, we don't live in a Disney story.

If there were one wish I could make come true, it would be for people to actually spend time understanding the issues, not simply accepting the spin, that people would stop living by sound-bites and start listening to what's really happening in the world.

Sound bites can make so many ugly things sound wonderful. The South American jungle has become the "Rain Forest." Why? Because a jungle is a place with mosquitoes that spread malaria, and alligators and piranha that gnaw off your legs when you step into the nearest stream, while "rainforest" sounds like a place where Disney characters dance and sing in beautiful harmony. Mucky swampland is now "natural wetlands" and stewardesses are now "flight attendants." I'll never understand that last one.

The term "Liberal" has not done well lately in the polls, so it has become "Progressive." Who can argue with progress? A "Fairness Doctrine" is being considered in order to stifle one side of a political argument. It sounds great. Who can argue with fairness? Except that in this case, fairness is really curbing our freedom of speech by limiting how much speech one side may have on the radio in favor of what those in power want you to hear.   Before you respond, keep in mind that this "Fairness Doctrine" does not apply to television, newspapers, or any other form of media except radio, the one where the opposite political party has more supporters.

Anyway, as I stated earlier, at our firm, a primary goal is to get agents through the teenage-like years and move them into the productive-adult phase of their careers. Perhaps it's time our entire society moved out of the teenage years and into a mature part of our lifecycle.

Oh, Stick a Fork in Your Eye

One of the greatest benefits of my team at Century 21 Keim has been how much fun the group is. We've been known to kid each other and play pranks which perhaps, once in a great while, have been taken a little too far.

A few years ago, our receptionist, who incidentally happens to be related to me, accidentally stuck a fork in her eye. No, I'm not exaggerating; she accidentally stuck a fork in her eye.

Life Lessons:

1. A great work environment must include a little fun.

2. Be careful with utensils!

Apparently she was eating and talking at the same time and somehow missed her mouth. I'm still not sure how that's possible, but at the time, I took care to remind myself of the fact that I've done many dumb things in my life as well.

A few weeks after her return, after making a complete recovery, Joe, who you're reading quite a bit about in this book, came into the office with gauze wrapped around his head, and one eye covered with a patch out of which was sticking, of all things, a plastic fork.

I can't remember ever laughing quite that hard.

An Uncomfortable Halloween

Each year, my wife and I host a Halloween party, which is costume optional, for our agents and friends. My wife does her best to put together a unique mix of appetizers, snacks and desserts, while I cater to the tasks of decorating and mixing exotic drinks. A few years ago, we realized that we spent so much time serving food and cleaning up, that we rarely had time to actually talk to our guests. So that year we elected to look for a few people to help.

An agent from our Allentown office, who we'll refer to as Peg in order to avoid any needless embarrassment, called to let us know that her daughter would be available to assist with setup and serving. Her daughter was in her twenties, but had a very youthful appearance. We agreed and asked that her daughter

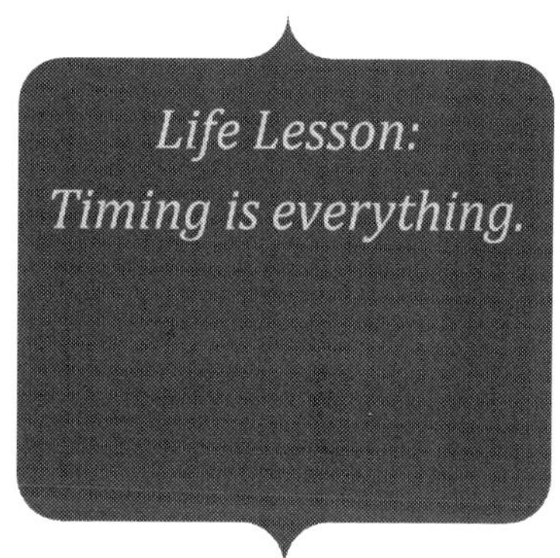

stop by our home a couple hours early to help prepare. When Peg asked if the girl could wear a costume, it never occurred to me to ask what kind.

A few hours before the party, my wife left to pick up all the last minute prepared foods from various vendors, and I was putting up cobwebs and scary pictures around the house when my ex-wife, Jennifer, stopped by to help with setup.

Minutes after she arrived, the front doorbell rang and Jennifer answered the front door to find what appeared to be a sixteen year old girl standing on the porch wearing a Catholic school girl outfit, complete with spike heels, a bare mid-rift, very small tied top, and a 7 or 8 inch skirt that left virtually nothing to the imagination.

"What the hell is this? Who are you?" Jennifer demanded. In answer to which, the girl, catching sight of me, simply smiled, pointed and said, "I'm here for him."

Some days it simply doesn't pay to get out of bed.

The Crazy Things Realtors Do

We've had our share of challenging realtors. They interview well and appear to be perfectly normal, but it sometimes seems that, once they start work, poof, they go crazy.

Some of the people attracted to the real estate industry are those that have failed at every other career they've tried. I guess they just want to prove one more time what they can do wrong. We try to avoid hiring these individuals, but are not always successful. Interviewing prospective employees is an art form that I have not perfectly mastered.

For example, as I was sitting in the conference room with several agents, including my mother, when an individual with our firm came up behind me and struck me in the head with a stiletto heel, causing blood to pour down my face. It's quite interesting when one is injured, looking out at the shocked faces looking back at you.

This was early in my career, and the group was joking about the dynamics of marriage. The woman in question, who was not in the room and therefore not part of the discussion, misheard what was said, thinking it was about her, and became enraged. I calmly turned back, with blood pooling on my shirt and trousers, and asked "*Why* did you do that?"

Some of our other gems over the years have included an agent who had significant Vietnam flashbacks which sent him running around the office, screaming in terror, while another, claiming that her son had been killed in an automobile accident, had all of us in a panic, trying to console her, only to discover that, not only was her son fine, but that she had used this ploy before to gain attention.

Needless to say, these agents did not remain long with us.

On the other hand, there are the agents who become so absorbed in what they are doing that they make what can be, at times, amusing mistakes. One of our most successful agents, Ellie, was driving me to a listing appointment for a luxury property. We were going over last minute ideas for how to approach the marketing of the property and she completely missed a new traffic light that was installed. I grabbed the seat and said "Ellie! You just ran a red light!"

"Where?" She shouted, slamming on the breaks and throwing us so rapidly into reverse that she backed through the same red light. Technically, I guess, we ran it twice.

Alcohol and Realtors...

Alcohol and selling real estate simply don't mix. Bob Wilfinger, our exceptionally gifted mortgage officer, came with us a few years ago to one of our Eastern Pennsylvania awards ceremonies at a very expensive hotel in Philadelphia.

As with all such big events, it was black tie, so Bob and I were both wearing those ruffled white shirts with little, decorative glass buttons. While I was introducing Bob to the Regional

Vice President of Century 21, a female agent from another firm stepped up and, telling Bob that he "smelled great," pulled his ruffled shirtfront open, and began to breathe deeply, sending a spray of little glass buttons across the room.

Alcohol and Realtors Part 2

Unfortunately, I'm probably the only half Irish guy in the world who can't handle his alcohol. An illustration of what I mean occurred when my staff and I went to a real estate convention in New Orleans about ten years ago.

On the first day, our title insurance agent, Deb Hartman, showed us around town. Although it was late February, it was warm in New Orleans, and I commented on being parched. Deb picked up something called a Magnum Hurricane, which appeared to be nothing more than a "slushy" to me, from a street vendor.

Since Pennsylvania is so careful about who can serve alcohol, who can serve it and at what time, I certainly did not expect this drink, which came in a forty-four ounce plastic cup from a corner vendor, complete with bendy-straw, to be alcoholic. In the time it took us to walk one block, I had slurped down every drop.

I don't remember much after that point, but I'm told by Tim Mahon and Wayne Taliber, who were with me at the time, that I, without warning, turned and walked out directly into traffic, and that they almost had to tackle me to keep me from being run over.

In the best-selling book, *Super Freakanomics*, the authors included a section indicating that an intoxicated individual may have more risk of being killed walking drunk than driving drunk, based on the percentage chance of death.[iii] I may actually be proof of their claim.

Incidentally, later on the same trip, I found myself on stage singing backup with the Spinners. Seated in the front row at the concert, Holly Weiss, another agent with our firm, and I were thrown on stage when the crowd surged forward during one of the final songs. Thankfully, the Spinners were very gracious and a lot of fun.

German Chocolate

While we're on the subject of alcohol, I might as well add that we all have to be careful about what we eat. Christa Klein, a kind-hearted colleague who emigrated from Germany many years ago, and who has been with us since our firm opened in 1986, brought back two four pound boxes of chocolate, after a recent visit to the country of her birth. Each was labeled in German and displayed photos of chocolate and small pieces of fruit.

Christa set one of the boxes on the counter of the agency's lobby, and knowing how fond I was of chocolate, left the other one on my desk.

Discovering the box when I returned from an appointment, I sampled the contents, one after the other, while I was absorbed in work on my computer. A quarter or half pound later, when I tried to stand, I discovered my head was swimming. Nevertheless, I stumbled into the outer office, only vaguely aware that I might have a problem.

To this day, I still do not know what I said, but apparently I offended one of our female agents so badly that she quit on the spot, left me a voice mail telling me that she was very unhappy with what I said, without actually stating *what* it was.

> *Life Lesson:*
> *Always read the label...*
> *or at least get someone to translate it.*

Only later did I discover that each one of the fine German chocolates contained about a shot of one hundred proof alcohol. I never had anything like them before, and thank goodness, will never have anything like them again. Christa has since explained that customs no longer allows her to bring these boxes with her for which I, for one, am extremely grateful.

Disclose Every Problem

Joe Bartera specializes in something called Buyer Agency, preferring to work with home buyers than home sellers. He has always been very careful to make sure he seeks out and discloses every potential problem with the house since he doesn't want a buyer to be stuck with a property that has issues.

While walking a client through a historic home a few years ago, listening to him tell us about some of the repairs and renovations that might have to be done in order to bring the house up to modern standards and codes, we noticed a broken window on the third floor.

Turning to the young couple, who were viewing the home, he told them that they would have to inspect the area around the window carefully because he wasn't sure how long the glass had been broken. Water could have seeped into the house, and settled between the walls.

As he continued to make his point, I saw a look of dismay settle on the face of the husband which was understandable, given that in taking such pains to draw our attention to the broken pane, he had inadvertently made certain that, sooner or later, we would all see the dead raccoon which lay on the floor below it.

Talk about unexpected consequences.

Foot in Mouth Syndrome

Tim Mahon is a broker who is famous for treating his clients well, always making certain that they understand what the situation is, and generous to a fault, a real "give you the shirt off my back" kind of guy.

In one case, a young woman, Becky, needed some electrical work and drywall repairs done in order to comply with FHA standards. And since she was already short on cash and couldn't afford to hire someone, Tim volunteered to assist her and when he spent a few afternoons completing the repairs, Becky was elated.

Unfortunately, however, she took his attention the wrong way, and apparently convinced that his intentions were romantic in nature, began to drop off gifts for him at the office, the most notable of which was a huge sheet cake, which, needless to say, we all participated in eating, only to discover that the top of the cake was a bit overdone and the bottom of the cake was still fairly raw. Either Becky's oven wasn't working correctly, or she broiled the cake. I'm not certain which.

This cake became the office joke of the week and, although I know now it was cruel, it certainly seemed funny at the time. And since Becky was not around, we thought there was no harm done.

The following week, I bounded down the steps from the second floor of my office to the front reception area and, without looking around, spied another sheet cake, carefully wrapped in saran wrap, on

> *Life Lesson: Never joke at the expense of another. It can be very hurtful, and ultimately, the joke may end up on you.*

the counter.

"Another of Becky's cakes?" I asked the receptionist. "No, don't tell me. I'll check for myself."

And lifting the cake about a foot off the counter, I dropped it and, hearing the uncooked bottom's sploosh sound, said "Yup, it's one of Becky's."

Only then, seeing the expression on the receptionist's face, did I realize that something was very wrong, and turning saw the lady in question directly behind me. The lesson I learned that day, one which I have never forgotten, is that we should never make jokes at someone else's expense.

Certainly, I will never forget the look on Becky's face.

Getting Feedback on Showings

Over the past two decades, I've been blessed to have some incredibly talented people work with me. Some of them have been real estate salespeople or brokers and some have been assistants, marketing personnel, receptionists and even programmers. However, I've also had my share of challenging employees over the years.

We once hired a young woman, who had a strong track record of delivering exceptional service to real estate clients, to handle our showing feedback and property advertising. She understood the marketing of homes, and she had five years experience assisting customers, so we were excited to have her on the team. What I didn't realize was that she might have issues with adult beverages until, that is, I received a call on a Tuesday morning from

Mr. Pradesh, the owner of several investment properties that we were currently marketing. Mr. Pradesh also owned a hotel, and many other investment properties that we were hoping to sell for him in the future.

"Mr. Keim, sir," he said. "I have a problem."

"I'm sorry to hear that, Mr. Pradesh. Tell me what it is and I'll do my best to correct it."

"Well, your assistant called me yesterday," he began.

Yesterday was Monday, the day my assistant called all of our clients to give them feedback on showings, so there seemed to be nothing unusual about that.

"Was she rude to you?" I asked, although I couldn't imagine that she would have been.

"No, she was very polite."

I waited for him to go on, and when he didn't, to fill the awkward gap, I proceeded to explain that we called with feedback in order to let owners know what clients liked and didn't like about their properties.

"Feedback helps us to assess how we're doing with each property," I said. "If twenty clients in a row tell us there's a problem, for example, then we know we may have an issue to correct. If you prefer that we don't give you feedback, I can stop, but I really believe it's a good thing to know what buyers think."

"I understand that," he said, "and I appreciate receiving calls."

"Well, then I'm not sure I completely understand what you're concerned about," I told him.

"Well, you see, she called me after work hours," he responded.

"Actually, that's wonderful," I replied, "because she took the time to get hold of those people she wasn't able to reach during the day, and conveyed information to them that they needed to have. I actually appreciate the fact that she worked after hours, and tried to make sure that our clients received the best possible service".

"I'm afraid that you don't understand," he said stiffly. "You see, she called me with feedback at one o'clock in the morning."

And sadly, as I later discovered, he was not the only one.

The Volkswagen Bug

My Uncle Sam worked with us briefly in the 1990's. His real name was Quentin Winslow, a regal name, but everyone called him Sam, a nickname somehow based on the San Quentin State Prison. After a string of bad luck and a few poor decisions, he was in a difficult spot financially. He was making do, but because he couldn't afford the sort of car that realtors usually chauffer clients around in, he decided he would work on listing appointments so that he could meet the clients at their homes.

One Saturday afternoon, when he was working at the office, trying to get some appointments to list homes, two women walked into the office and asked if they could be shown the area. It's rare that clients walk into a real estate company without an appointment, but it does happen from time to time.   In this case, Sam had no choice but to take them on their tour in his battered, 1970s vintage Volkswagen Beetle.

Life Lesson: Ask for help when you need it.

When they returned, not long after leaving, I watched from the window as he helped these well dressed, but sadly rumpled ladies extricate themselves from the back seat. When I opened the office door for them, I noticed that they seemed exhausted.

"You must have looked at a good many properties," I said, to which the taller of the two, an aristocratic looking woman whose clothing appeared to be particularly disheveled, replied that they had actually visited only two.

"We couldn't go on after that," the other told me, "because we could hardly walk."

It was, I thought, a curious comment to make, but one that Sam explained after they had hobbled off. It seemed that, because the back floor of his Volkswagen had been torn away, the ladies had been forced to hold their legs up as the pavement flashed by underneath.

"But they were good sports about it," he assured me cheerfully.

And perhaps that was the case, but it did not escape my notice that we never saw hide nor hair of them again.

Our Beloved Receptionist

This is probably the one story I shouldn't retell, but I laugh every time someone repeats it, so, dear reader, forgive me if I offend you. I'll begin by telling you about one of our long time receptionists, a young lady whom I'll refer to as Kay, who tended to overdramatize much of her life. At one point, having found her at her desk, sobbing, I asked her what was wrong, thinking someone must have died, only to find that she had just come back from the dentist.

"My teeth," she gasped, barely getting the words out, "my teeth are literally rotting out of my mouth."

Apparently, she had a couple of cavities. To Kay, this was a crisis of paramount importance in her life.

During the reconstruction phase of our Allentown office, we had packed the entire staff into one half of the building while the other half was demolished. Because the demolition was taking place during the winter, which in hindsight was not the brightest move I could have made, cold air leaked from every direction, so we had the room into which we were packed closed tight. Suddenly the door burst open and Kay appeared along with a gust of cold air, tears running down her cheeks.

"Loren," she cried. "I have to go home."

"What's wrong, Kay?" Theresa asked her.

"I'm having my period."

Theresa was dumbstruck for a minute, but quickly recovered. "And what is the issue?"

"I don't have any tampons!"

I think I turned bright red. One of my assistants, Mary Hudock, stood and said, "I have some pads in my purse."

Kay formed an "O" with her mouth and in her best version of Valley-girl talk, said, "*Hello.* I'm wearing a thong."

My other assistant, Brittany, laughed and said "Don't panic. I have tampons." She pulled one out of her purse and handed it to Kay.

Kay held it between two fingers and cocked a hip. "What am I supposed to do with this? Smoke it? This is *way* too small!"

Now I was five shades of red, being the only man in the room and highly embarrassed. It seemed like hours that everyone in the room gaped, open mouthed, at Kay. Theresa broke the silence. "Kay, there's a CVS a block up the street. Go get a box."

She left and didn't return for almost forty-five minutes. "I'm sorry I'm late. I had this huge blow-out with the manager of the CVS. Can you believe he actually wanted me to pay *first?* I told him it was an emergency, but he wouldn't listen. I told him what I thought of him."

On another occasion, Mary buzzed me from the first floor and quietly asked me to come downstairs right away. There was a problem, she said, but I had to see it first-hand. I bounded down the steps into the lobby and there was Kay, who despite the fact that she was wearing a mini skirt and this was an office, was sitting with one foot on her desk and the other on the floor. The client who was sitting facing her was clearly having a difficult time knowing where to look.

Needless to say shortly after that, Kay's association with the agency came, sadly, to an abrupt end.

Watch the Kids

Deb, a local title insurance agent and a good friend, had many get-togethers, picnics and parties at her home, which was perfectly set up for entertaining a large crowd, featuring as it did, a great room with vaulted ceiling, leading out to a family room with a gorgeous bar and a hot tub room. Downstairs was another pair of family rooms including one which contained a pool table. Outside, an enormous three level deck hovered over a patio, a sizable gazebo, an outdoor bar and an L-shaped in-ground pool.

At one such picnic for local realtors, a crowd of well over one hundred were drinking, eating, drinking, swimming and, of course, drinking, when an agent from a competing firm, who we'll refer to as Amy to avoid any litigation from the embarrassment my story may cause, arrived with her two children. And although the kids constituted a distinct minority, they enjoyed the food, music and pool while their mother spent a bit of time enjoying adult beverages and the company of other agents. I am not criticizing this choice by the way. I understand the need to relax.

By late in the evening, Amy, having shared many stories and many drinks with her compatriots, was not able to walk very steadily. In fact, she stumbled and fell on the lawn when she left her perch at the indoor bar. Shortly after that, she decided it was time to leave and collected her children.

"You can't let her leave!" my wife told me. "She can't drive those children in her condition."

I did my best to convince Amy that someone should drive her home, and she would hear nothing of it. She needed her mini-van for clients in the morning and was not leaving it behind. When my wife suggested that I drive Amy and her kids home in the mini-van with Theresa following in our car, Amy reluctantly agreed.

It took both of us to propel her into the car. Once the children were safely packed into the back seat, we were on our way. Unfortunately our problems were not completely over since our intoxicated friend now became extremely affectionate, putting one arm around my shoulders and telling me that Theresa and I were her very, very best friends. I could only guess what my wife, driving close behind us, must be thinking.

Things could however, be even worse, as I soon discovered when we reached her home, and still embracing me, she managed to manipulate the garage door opener. As the door rose, there, standing in the headlights, was a man I assumed to be her husband, arms crossed on his considerable chest, wearing an expression that made me think that it would be quite possible for him to do me some sort of bodily harm.

So much, I thought, for being a Good Samaritan.

Putting the van in park halfway down the driveway, I hopped out, waved at him and hot-footed it back to Theresa's car.

As far as I am concerned, in matters such as these caution outweighs valor every single time.

Salespeople!

One of the other challenges of managing and working with real estate agents is that the best ones are often in 'sales mode,' trying to persuade everyone around them to agree with their ideas, or to side with them in an argument. As I've mentioned, election years are a lot of fun. This characteristic is not limited, however, to real estate sales.

Sadly, I am the recipient of hundreds of calls each year from mortgage brokerage salespeople, title insurance agents, insurance salespeople and home inspectors who want business, as well as representatives of every office product, advertising media and software product known to mankind. Some of them are very difficult to get off the phone without being rude and hanging up.

Some of the more interesting salespeople are the dreaded yellow page representatives. Each fall, I am visited by several 'consultants' representing all the various yellow page directories claiming that thousands of clients will magically appear if I just spend a few thousand dollars advertising with them. Yet, they typically refuse to leave copies of any of the information and statistics they flash quickly past me.

Last year, one of the yellow page directories was represented by an attractive twenty-something young woman who showed up on a cold October day wearing a skirt and a blouse cropped to expose several inches of belly. This was a surprise both because I thought the representative should have been more professionally dressed and because the weather was awfully cold for this outfit.

Sitting down at the conference room table, she looked at me and said "Oh my, you're really cute."

Although men generally love to hear compliments, I'm an overweight forty-something guy and am not a complete idiot. "I like your tie" would have been a much more realistic compliment. I wondered how many small business owners fell for that line.

She opened her briefcase, pulling out the latest advertising statistics, and then paused to hold up her left hand. She looked at her hand and then back up at me. "Gee, I'm sorry. I'm used to looking down at my wedding ring, but I'm not married anymore. I'm single and available."

I asked her to leave.

Chapter 7:
Paradigms: How we perceive reality

An individual's paradigm is how they perceive the reality around them. Many of us are so ingrained in our beliefs that we can't see or accept any viewpoint that doesn't match our own. In fact, in our country and our world, there are people who have diametrically opposing viewpoints, both of which they believe are correct.

This is often a challenge when negotiating a sales contract. A home seller absolutely believes he has the nicest home in the entire tri-state area and that he is selling it too cheaply. The typical buyer believes the same home needs renovation and is overpriced. In both cases, the client thinks that if the agent were to simply explain their reality to the other party, they would accept it.

The Express Lane

An example of this sort of paradigm can be found in the express lane of any local supermarket.

There have been many times when I am running late to get to an appointment, a meeting, home to see the kids or attend a family get together, and for whatever reason, need to stop at the grocery store and pick up something. Understandably, I go to the express lane where a customer cannot take more than ten items.

Invariably, there is someone in front of me who has approximately six thousand four hundred and eight items, and because ever other aisle is full, I need to wait until her transaction is complete. And, as if that were not enough of an inconvenience, as soon as she finishes her transaction, she begins a conversation with the cashier regarding something they might have in common.

"Really?" The checkout clerk responds happily. "Well, my kids did this and that too. This year they're going to do some other thing!"

"That's fantastic," responds the patron. "Did I tell you about my daughter, Alex?"

At this point, I usually want to reach out and strangle both of them. Please don't misunderstand me. I'm usually a calm, collected and fairly harmless person. Even when I've been in some pretty stressful situations, I've managed to maintain my cool.   As I pointed out earlier in this book, I've been shot at and remained calm.

> *Life Lesson: Always be considerate of those around you.*

This sort of lack of consideration, however, absolutely drives me crazy. After all, I'm in a hurry, which is why I only picked up a few items and why I'm standing in the lane that has the big red sign labeled, "Express Lane: 10 Items or Less."

I cannot, for the life of me, understand why these two people need to be holding a conversation when one should be working and the other should be heading out to her car with her overabundance of groceries which she should not have purchased in the express lane in the first place. It makes perfect sense to me that I should want to throttle both of them.

My wife, on the other hand, will simply say, "Isn't that wonderful?"

My head snaps back toward my wife so quickly, I nearly dislodge the bones in my neck. I'm in shock. "What do you mean wonderful?" I gasp. "You're being sarcastic, right?"

"Of course I'm not being sarcastic," she'll reply. "It is wonderful that, in times like these, people can still take time to really communicate."

Theresa, you see, really believes in the fundamental goodness of everyone, a philosophy which drives me nuts, too. But that's another story. She believes that some people's ability to connect with each other and communicate is a wonderful fundamental character trait. The fact that because of this I'm going to be late getting somewhere and potentially have someone angry with me for my tardiness strikes her as incidental.

I, on the other hand, am far more concerned with people's lack of consideration for others, particularly me.

Homeowners Versus Mortgage Companies

I first experienced the challenge of dealing with tenants when I purchased a townhome on 14th Street in Allentown. I was a young realtor, at the time, struggling to make a living and pay my bills and had purchased a rental property because I thought it would help me to increase my income. After a few unexpected repairs and tenants who were slow to

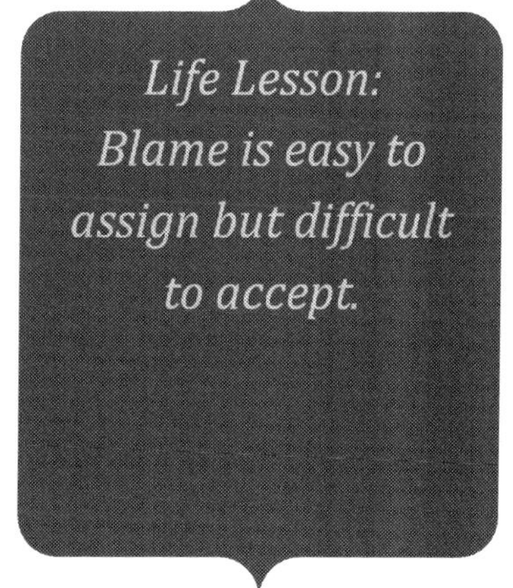

pay their rent, I realized that I would probably lose money on this building forever. In fact, I would probably have to work longer hours simply to pay the losses on this rental property.

During the summer of my second year as a landlord, the current tenant lost his job. He was struggling to provide for his family, but so was I. He asked me not to evict him for thirty days so that he could find another job, one that would allow him to catch up on his payments. I reluctantly agreed and received partial payment for July and August.   September and October went by with no payment at all, and since the mortgage on that house was equivalent to the one on my own, the situation was causing me and my wife a good deal of stress.

By November, I realized I had been too lenient by far. My renters now owed four and a half months rent which meant that I couldn't continue paying the mortgage on the house they were living in. I asked my assistant Michelle to give them a last courtesy call and let them know that I was serious about my last correspondence to the effect that I was going to file an eviction notice with the magistrate.

I came back to the office a few hours later to find Michelle, who has a heart of gold, having heard the same sad story that the tenant had given me, had gone out and bought him and his family a Christmas tree. I, of course, was livid.

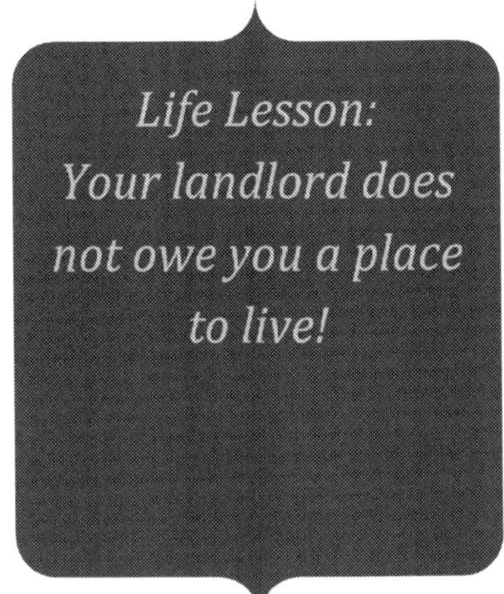

"Don't you understand these people are ruining my credit and possibly driving me into bankruptcy?" I asked her. "There are hundreds of jobs in the local paper and in nearly five months, he hasn't been able to find *anything!*"

The tenant's perspective was that if I owned rental property and had my name on real estate signs, I must be rich, so it's only right that I give him a break. Michelle's perspective was that if I filed eviction just before Thanksgiving, the tenant might be thrown out before Christmas. My perspective was that I had given these tenants far more time to pay their rent than was reasonable, particularly when I was struggling to pay my own family's bills. What kind of Christmas would I be able to give my *own* family?

Since that experience, our firm has managed hundreds of rental units and regularly receives calls from tenants who truly believe it's our *obligation* to let them remain where they are until they find work. The owners, who we represent, feel very differently and are not always understanding if we don't move swiftly to rectify the situation.

Many home owners feel the same way when dealing with their mortgage lenders. In the spring of 2009, the activist group Acorn broke into the home of Donna Hanks in Baltimore, Maryland that had been foreclosed by the lender and reinstated the former owner, challenging the establishment to evict her again and take legal action against them.[iv] The view they appear to spin is that the evil mortgage company gave the former owner the mortgage money to purchase the home only so that they could take the home away for themselves. Incidentally, according to news reports, Donna Hanks purchased the home for $87.000 and then somehow refinanced it for $270,000 and failed to pay the mortgage.[v] Where did the money go?

In the case of the mortgage company, whether they are a conglomerate or the small local bank around the corner, they do not want to own your home for the simple reason that collecting mortgages is their bread and butter. That's why they immediately sell the home, and generally take a bath on the mortgage money they have loaned the consumer. Certainly there were unscrupulous lenders during the huge boom of 2003 to 2006, who thought they could write loans and sell those loans off quickly in the secondary market in order to turn a quick profit.

The truth, however, is that borrower's loan is probably not owned by the lender. It may be serviced by the mortgage company, but actually owned, as part of a mortgage backed security, by someone else. That mortgage could be part of your company's retirement program, your sister's 401K or an investment by your community's school district. If the borrower doesn't pay the mortgage, then you must pay it by losing the money you effectively loaned them. Which is fair?

Although Acorn has done a considerable job helping the less fortunate in many communities, it is also the same group that was accused of threatening mortgage lenders several years ago for not loaning enough money to low income households and minorities. At that point, they appeared to believe that lenders should reduce lending restrictions in order to allow more people to own homes. Now they believe the lenders took advantage of these people by giving them loans they couldn't afford, which is, in my opinion, an interesting shift in the group's own paradigm.

However, I'm not giving a free pass to lenders. I've written some scathing articles and even a book about the mortgage meltdown, which includes advice on how to negotiate with your lender. However, it's interesting to see the picketing and the anger by people who borrowed the money, promised to pay it back over time and then failed to do so. Of course, many of these borrowers lost their jobs and could no longer afford the payments. Some didn't even understand the documentation. However, given the nature of the capitalistic society of which we have every right to be so proud, we are all expected to pay for what we get because otherwise the system would break down.

Ultimately, I sold the property on 14th Street the following year, when my new tenant, an Allentown firefighter and ex-marine, was shot in the face in front of the home.[vi]

Off to Jail

In the mid 1990's, our firm, Century 21 Keim Realtors, began receiving mortgage company offers that appeared to be too good to be true. At that time, mortgage programs that offered low down payments and would still allow buyers to purchase homes with relatively low credit scores were just beginning to appear. These loans came at the price of a high interest rate. If the lender was going to take the risk of loaning a lot of money to a borrower with limited qualifications, the borrower would have to pay a premium for that money. Later programs allowed nearly anyone to take advantage of low interest loans.

Several of our clients took advantage of these programs and eventually, after paying on the loan for a year or two and establishing a payment history, which allowed them to refinance at lower rates. As lenders started reducing restrictions and offering great loan products to buyers, we used those products instead.

In the late 1990's, I received a call from a reporter who wanted me to give him a quote before he fried me in the press by claiming that our firm had intentionally injured a client by allowing them to take a higher-than-normal interest rate loan, with the result that a family was now at risk of being thrown out into the street because we had allowed "predatory lenders" to take advantage of the couple.

I explained to the reporter that the buyer had poor credit and no down payment and that the interest rate they had paid was three percent over the prevailing rate at that time. The facts were that the buyer was getting into a home with virtually no money out of pocket and a payment of less than $650 per month and since to rent a home, like the one they purchased, would probably cost $750 per month or more, they were actually able to own a home cheaper than they could rent one, and without any money down.

To put it briefly, they were paying a premium in order to try to earn a piece of the American dream. Too many people in the country now expect everything to be given to them. The lender's premium on the mortgage rate was simply a function of the risk the lender was taking in even writing the loan for this borrower. I stressed the fact that the buyer had actually purchased the home for less per month than they would have paid in rent, and added the fact that the buyer wasn't able to pay the mortgage, not because the payment was too high, but because the buyer had gone to prison on charges of armed robbery.

The reporter was shocked that there actually was another side to the story and that it couldn't easily be spun as mortgage company greed, and having found another story to support his contentions, ran that one instead.

A Brief Explanation of the Mortgage Crisis

In 1990, approximately 64.2% of Americans owned their own homes. Lenders carefully selected who would receive mortgages based on a few key indicators of their ability to repay the loans. In the real estate industry, we called these indicators the four "C's". They include credit worthiness, capital, collateral and capacity.

Credit worthiness is critical to making sure a loan is repaid. If the borrower doesn't have a decent credit score, it shows they have not paid their bills on time. If the borrower isn't paying their bills now, what would make a lender believe they will become better at paying those bills once they own a home? Capital is also important. In business, it's called having skin-in-the-game. Lenders don't want to loan the entire amount of a purchase, because the buyer or borrower doesn't have anything invested in the purchase. If their situation changes, it is easier for the buyer or borrower to walk away because they don't really have anything, other than their credit rating to lose.

Collateral means that the home simply has to be worth what the buyer is paying for it. A lender doesn't want to risk having to take back a property and re-sell it if there isn't enough equity to sell the home in the case of default. Finally, capacity means the borrower has to have an income that allows them to make the payments. Lenders carefully determined whether or not the borrower had the ability to make the payments by assessing how long the borrower had been employed and what percentage of their income could be used to make the mortgage payment.

This system of carefully screening candidates for mortgages worked effectively in keeping the number of foreclosures very low for most of the last century. During the 1990's, the Community Reinvestment Act (CRA) was used to pressure lenders to reduce restrictions on the qualifications of buyers in order to increase the number of home owners, and particularly to assist minorities and low-income home buyers in purchasing homes. In fact, in 1999, the *New York Times* reported that Fannie Mae and Freddie Mac were "under increasing pressure from the Clinton Administration to expand mortgage loans among low and moderate income people."[vii]

Fannie Mae and Freddie Mac are the eight hundred pound gorillas in the lending industry, purchasing more than half of the mortgage loans made by lenders. These quasi-government agencies set the rules for lending practices in the United States. Their direction changed in 1992 when a Housing Bill was passed that set a goal for Fannie Mae and Freddie Mac to have 30% of their home loans given to low and moderate income households.

In 1996, that number was raised to 40% and then raised again to 42% in 1997. Fannie Mae and Freddie Mac, collectively called Government Sponsored Entities, or GSEs, needed to find a way to loan more money to their target group. In order to facilitate this, they gave preferential treatment to mortgage companies and lenders who reduced their underwriting criteria. Lenders signed a "Declaration of Fair Lending Principals and Practices."[viii]

All this boils down to the fact that these quasi-government institutions were the largest buyer of loans, and they actively reduced the restrictions required for obtaining a mortgage. Most lenders followed suite in order to take advantage of writing more loans and selling them to these institutions.

Programs became available, through Fannie Mae and Freddie Mac lenders and through Subprime lenders, offering 100% financing, 103% financing and in some cases, up to 125% financing. The supposed logic behind this idea was that buyers had decent credit and stable jobs but weren't able to save any money, so why not loan them the entire amount? Unfortunately, it also means that these home buyers had little or no money put into the property, and therefore, little to lose by walking away. It also left no equity for a lender if the buyer defaulted on the mortgage.

Even that wasn't enough, however. Programs were created that allowed borrowers to state their income on applications rather than actually provide proof of their earnings. In this case, the logic was that self employed people didn't show all their income, or couldn't prove it readily, so these individuals could not be turned away. The lender would simply charge them a slightly higher interest rate than the norm for the privilege of "stating" their income.

Lower and lower credit requirements continued to push the pool of potential home buyers into the depths of the unqualified, simply because the checks and balances of the mortgage industry were totally out of whack with reality. Low interest rates, combined with low or no down payments and easy credit with very few verifications is a recipe for mortgage disaster. Even worse, the executives of these government sponsored entities received hundreds of millions of dollars in bonuses and salaries for increasing home ownership and lending to so many borrowers.

In many cases, however, there were conservative lenders who were unwilling to follow these new reduced guidelines with the result that many of them were threatened or sued by community action groups claiming that segments of the population were being discriminated against by archaic rules. Most lenders gave in, rather than go through the negative publicity and legal costs associated with continuing along a more conservative path.

Part of the dramatic rise in home prices was directly attributable to the rise in home ownership. From 1993 to 2005, the percentage of Americans who owned homes jumped from approximately 63% to approximately 69.2%, an increase that was accounted for by the fact that most of those new homeowners were first time buyers.

In any given year, approximately 8-10% of the population purchases a home, and a little better than a third of those buyers are first time home buyers. When the number of first time home buyers began to increase, the huge demand for first time homes drove the prices up. Those sellers then relocated into "move-up" homes, creating another category of significant demand. Finally, owners of moderate homes, who had never planned to move again, reconsidered, finding what constituted their "dream homes" to be within reach.   The increasing prices of moderate housing, combined with historically low interest rates created an opportunity to move to a luxury property that many people never expected to achieve.

Ultimately, the combination of easy credit, low interest rates, high affordability, low unemployment and high immigration all coalesced to create one of the highest periods of home appreciation in history. Like all good things, as we know now, this too had to end.

In September of 2003, because the White House had become concerned about lending policies, Treasury Secretary John Snow went before Congress to propose a regulatory agency to oversee Fannie Mae and Freddie Mac, but Fannie Mae donated large sums of money to key people in congress, and no oversight was established. Congressman Barney Frank actually claimed that "Fannie Mae and Freddie Mac are not in a crisis," and that Fannie and Freddie needed to do even more to increase home ownership in America.[ix]

When hearings occurred in 2004 and 2005, a second attempt to regulate Fannie Mae and Freddie Mac was also blocked. Congresswoman Maxine Waters stated that they were trying to, "fix something that frankly wasn't broke," and that "we do not have a crisis at Freddie Mac and particular at Fannie Mae."[x]

I submit that if these programs had not allowed unqualified home buyers to purchase homes, the housing recession would not have been nearly as severe as it has been. Foreclosures would not be reaching their current levels, and it is unlikely that housing prices would have dipped as low as they have.

Again, please don't misunderstand me. Giving buyers the chance at home ownership is an admirable thing, but it has to be done with sensible rules that won't destroy our country and our way of life. Forcing the banking system to give away money to anyone and then propping up the losses with government backing by raising taxes is not the answer.

I am also not entirely blaming the Federal Government. There is plenty of blame to go around. Mortgage brokers made money in fees by writing loans and some ignored signs that a borrower would not be able to pay the mortgage. Appraisers earned fees by estimating the value of homes for those mortgage brokers and some may have been influenced by lenders to inflate appraisals. Financial institutions made money packaging the loans and selling them to Fannie Mae or selling them as mortgage backed securities. Even Wall Street Rating Agencies made money by rating the mortgage backed securities. There is plenty of guilt to go around, but it starts with government intervention.

The mortgage system is broken and needs to be fixed by people that are not part of the problem, rather than a congress that must assume much of the blame for our current economic situation

Dr. Thode and Ursula the Bar Girl

Explaining the mortgage meltdown leads me to another interesting story. I was part of a workshop at Lehigh University this year at which the speaker, Dr. Stephen Thode, was trying to explain the collapse of the financial industry by using the analogy of Ursula, a German bar owner, who built her business by allowing her patrons to buy drinks on credit without taking any cash up front.

Life Lesson: Stop taking offense. Relax. Life is too short already

The patrons received drinks and in return, gave I.O.U.s for their outstanding bar tabs. Since patrons could open tabs without paying anything up front, customers flocked from far and wide.

These I.O.U.s were then used as collateral to mortgage her bar and buy her supplies. The bank, where she took out her loans, then sold the loans by securitizing them and selling them on Wall Street. Of course, the bar patrons never paid, causing the owner to declare bankruptcy and push the bar into foreclosure, which is exactly what happened with subprime mortgages.

Ultimately, the bar losses were paid by the government, just as has been the case in the current housing crisis, which funded these losses by taking money from non-drinkers. Those who were responsible with their money and the amounts they borrowed are now paying, through taxes, for everybody who was irresponsible, including banks, Wall Street and the borrowers.

Dr. Thode's presentation featured comical representations of the players. For example, the bankers were the Three Stooges, and the bar owner was represented by a photograph of a waitress in a cute, German barmaid costume, carrying a pint of lager.

"That's sexist! The photo objectifies women." a woman in the audience protested after the speech.

Why, I wondered, are people so easily perturbed? Certainly the photograph did not show us a woman flaunting her sexuality, but only someone doing her job.

I've heard many women complain angrily that there are double standards for men and women. There probably are. But in the case of clothing, women seem to wear whatever they want, whenever they want, and men are supposed not to notice or comment.

Men and women see situations differently in many respects. Men are visually stimulated by looking at pretty women. It is, quite simply, a fact of life. Women realize this and often wear clothing that is designed to attract a man's attention. Does anyone really believe that so many women have slightly bare mid-rifts and pierced belly buttons because that is more comfortable?

To be fair, I've heard a number of women state that they simply wear short skirts, low cut tops, bare bellies and low rise jeans with thongs simply because these clothes make them feel good about themselves but in my opinion, that is simple horse pucky.

Getting back to my original point, wear whatever you want, but be careful when you accuse men of objectifying women, because the standard for these "looks" are often created by women.

Using the System

If you're easily offended, you may want to skip over this short essay. About a decade ago, a tall, well-built, muscular man spoke with my wife about purchasing a home. It was, he explained, a delicate matter since the woman he was living with was not actually his wife, and he wanted to make sure that his purchase would not affect the income she presently received from the government in the form of welfare payments.

He had received information about a series of grant programs that would allow him to purchase a home with no money down, using grants from government agencies and receive a grant to fix up the property from the city of Allentown. The renovation grant could actually be forgiven in five years if he stayed in the property. Theresa confirmed that the programs were currently in existence.

Life Lesson: The system is not always fair. Carefully choose which battles you wish to wage.

However, when it came to the qualification process, we discovered that he was forty-something and hadn't worked in twenty years. According to the buyer, he moved to America over twenty years before, worked a couple years legally and then developed a nervous condition and was given social security. He laughed as he told us this story, but I was not amused. First, this gentleman looked like he was in much better physical shape than I, and he wasn't working. Second, was social security *really* set up to fund people with "nervous conditions" who weren't even natural born citizens?

Since the disability income was permanent, he was able to count it toward obtaining a mortgage. He stayed unmarried in order to preserve "his wife's" income, which he thought could also be counted toward the purchase. In addition, their seventeen or eighteen year old daughter, who was planning to live with them, was now receiving welfare because she had a one year old child.

The client selected homes to see, and Theresa scheduled them. Although this man didn't make my wife nervous, he made *me* nervous, so I went along with them to view homes. In the car, he told a few jokes and then turned serious as we arrived in center city. Turning to my wife, he said "Theresa, if you ever want to see the other side of life, you can come down here with me. Never come by yourself, because we don't like you Americans down here."

I was floored. Here's a guy living in our country for more than two decades, living on our system and tax dollars telling us he doesn't like Americans. I said nothing.

After two days of searching, he selected a home and when Theresa explained that he needed a deposit to hold it, even if he ultimately purchased with no money down, he said it would be no problem, pulling a wad of bills out of his pocket. He peeled off ten one-hundred dollar bills, leaving me with the distinct impression that he was working under the table somewhere. In any event, he applied for the mortgage and started the process of inspections of the home.

About two weeks later, he called to let us know he had found a better house and wanted to get out of the original agreement of sale. And when Theresa explained that if he did that, he would lose his deposit because there was no way out of the contract other than being denied by the mortgage company or finding something catastrophically wrong on the building inspection report, he told her in no uncertain terms that he wanted his thousand dollars back *and* his mortgage application fee back and that he intended to have it.

The next day, he surprised us at the office when he arrived with his attorney, a pro bono legal counselor, whose first words were "Who explained this contract to my client?"

"I did," I told him, "and I covered it completely."

"Do you speak fluent [his native language]?" Not knowing where this conversation was going, I replied with an "I can get by."

"My client doesn't speak a word of English, so how exactly did you explain it to him? Did you have a translator?"

"He speaks perfect English," I replied, jumping to my feet, livid. "He was telling us jokes in the car."

"Not according to us." The attorney, who I had met before, explained to me that we were going to refund this money or they would be dragging us through the press as a company prepared to take advantage of a minority client. I certainly do not discriminate, and I pointed out that several of our top agents, who were my good friends, were of Latino descent or Middle Eastern descent and he'd have a really hard time proving that our agency discriminated.

When he continued to stress the fact that the press would love this story, I pointed out that I didn't even have the buyer's money and couldn't give it back even if I wanted to since in Pennsylvania the money is held in escrow by the seller's agent or attorney. In order to have it released, both parties have to reach an agreement as to who gets the deposit, or a judge has to issue an order to that effect.

"I'm not asking for the money to be released from escrow," he said matter-of-factly. "I'm telling you that you will pay this man what he put out or I will take you to court. I don't have to tell you that, when I do, it will cost you so much in legal bills that you may lose your company."

In my mind, these tactics represented an extortion attempt, and although I paid it, I swore that I never would again. The anger I felt then is still raw today, ten years later.

Incidentally, I am not raging against immigration. What has made America the world's melting pot has been the great migrations of immigrants seeking the American Dream. In fact, some of the most accomplished individuals in our nation have been first or second generation immigrants. Inventor Albert Einstein, former Secretary of State Madeline Albright, Governor Arnold Schwartzenegger, Joseph Pulitzer and race car driver Mario Andretti, who lives in my area, are a very small sample of those born outside the United States.

Sadly, there are times I feel that families moving to this country are more motivated to success than natural born citizens. My friend, Francisco, moved to the United States from Peru and over the past two decades has always seemed to have at least two careers and is continually expanding his knowledge through education and hard work.

My concern is directed at those who move to take advantage of the system rather than to build a better life for their families.

Tolerance and Intolerance

Speaking of differing paradigms, why is it that we need to be tolerant of the intolerant? Many of the same individuals who rally together for peace, believing we can solve the Middle East crisis with love and respect seem to spout the most venomous forms of hatred with those that disagree with them. Soldiers protecting our country are portrayed, by those who preach tolerance, to be murdering savages, raping and pillaging in foreign lands to please our expansionist war-mongering leaders, in their eternal quest for power and oil.

One of our agents was recently accosted because of a bumper sticker on his car. The sticker, which came with the car when he purchased it, read "If you can read this, thank a teacher. If you are reading this in English, thank a soldier." A neighbor of one of our listings marched into the home to loudly protest that this "heinous" sticker was on the car. He strongly suggested that our client cancel their listing because our agent was condoning hate speech.

How in the world is thanking a teacher for their good works and thanking a soldier for helping protect our nation considered 'hate speech?'

Another case in point was the 2009 Miss USA pageant.   In 2009, Carrie Prejean was crowned Miss California and nearly won the Miss USA pageant. Whatever you may think of her on a personal level, her score was radically diminished when she answered the question of whether or not she would support same sex marriage.

When Carrie answered honestly that she believes a marriage is between a man and a woman, open hostility erupted around her, despite the fact that she only disagrees with one part of the gay agenda. Groups worked feverishly to have her crown removed as Miss California, and she has received a torrent of hate mail. One of the pageant judges was quoted as saying, "I would have ripped the crown off her head." Why the intolerance of her beliefs?

Before my own hate mail starts piling in, let me preface my remarks with the fact that I'm not a proponent of same sex marriage but that I am not against it either. I have no opinion at this point, and I'm simply trying to use this subject for an example of the other side of intolerance. I have several gay friends and my former brother-in-law's brother, who is a great guy, is gay. I even did photography at his wedding.

I believe that any monogamous union should allow the partners to have rights.   One side sees marriage, or the act of holy matrimony, as a religious term which precludes this coupling. The other side sees it as a legal right. I am no expert. Is marriage a legal term or a religious term? Is it a religious rite or a legal right? I don't know the answer, but some very bright individuals have coined the term "civil unions" to attempt to appease both sides of the argument, and hopefully provide the same rights as marriage. It hasn't worked.

Regardless of what term is used for this type of union, and what rights the term conveys, why is so much hate directed at anyone who disagrees with the gay marriage position? Why can't we respect the beliefs and opinions of all sides, or simply agree to disagree?

What does the question have to do with being Miss USA? That judge explained that Miss USA must represent the views of *all* Americans, not just one side. That's not possible because the country is made up of different viewpoints.

In another situation, the Freedom From Religion Foundation has done everything possible to short circuit a U.S. postage stamp with a rendering of Mother Teresa on it. Their claim is that, despite Mother Teresa being one of the greatest humanitarians in history and a tireless worker on behalf of the poor in third world nations, the fact that she was also a Catholic nun should disqualify her. Her religious views are supposedly her "darker side," which particularly included her "antiabortion ideology."[xi]

Perhaps I'm speaking too frankly, but it always seems to me that those who claim to "celebrate diversity" or "celebrate religious choice" and rage that conservatives are intolerant can sometimes be the most intolerant of individuals. They want everyone to tolerate their lifestyles, and their opinions, while telling those who disagree that they are racist, sexist, or homophobes.

What I'm trying to get across is that there are two sides to most issues. Just because someone believes in traditional values does not mean that they are bigots. It has gotten to the point that we are afraid to speak our minds because the political correctness crowd will show up at our homes with torches and pitchforks. If we're to have an open debate on any issue, it must be done without one side assuming they are correct and labeling the other side as hate-mongers.

Tenants... 'Nuff Said

Many landlords and realtors consider tenant selection to be something of an art-form because it is so difficult to determine whether a prospective tenant is going to actually pay the rent. In one case recently, a tenant interviewed very well, and although his credit was shaky, he had a strong explanation based on an illness and challenges at work. When my assistant, Keri, called to let the tenant know the landlord had approved his application, she was greeted by a voice mail message that informed anyone who listened that this individual was screening calls, would not answer blocked phone numbers, and knew he was behind with every creditor on earth and they should all give up because he wasn't paying.

If a prospective tenant's credit is 'so-so', we call the prior landlord to verify that the tenant paid in a timely manner. What we've discovered is that many landlords will lie in order to get rid of a bad tenant because a voluntary move-out is cheaper and faster than an eviction.

"Sure, they are great! I'm sorry to see them go," we might hear. When the truth is closer to "I haven't seen a rent check in ninety days, and the four cats they're not supposed to have living in the property have sprayed in every corner of the home meaning we'll have to fumigate for weeks. "

One of my competitors, Rudy Amelio, came up with a simple solution to verify whether or not tenants have paid in the past. He requires them to produce the cancelled checks for the last year. He's not worried if they have a few late credit card bills on their credit, as long as they pay their rental payments.

On one occasion, Rudy asked clients for copies of their cancelled checks, only to be told that they generally paid by cash or money order.

"We get receipts, though," the prospecting tenant announced.

They returned to his office several hours later to show twelve completed rental receipts, each written on the due date of the rent.

Sadly, each was also sequentially numbered starting at '001.' They had likely gone to the closest Office Depot or Staples and purchased a receipt book, and without realizing the receipts were numbered, simply wrote out the first twelve.

Sand in the Living Room

Tenants are also often a source of frustration and expense for landlords, realtors and property managers. I am continually amazed at how many tenants will move out and leave behind several dressers, a bed, an old television, lots of clothing and children's toys. This is something I can't quite comprehend. Why leave these items behind? Clean-outs are a regular occurrence for property managers.

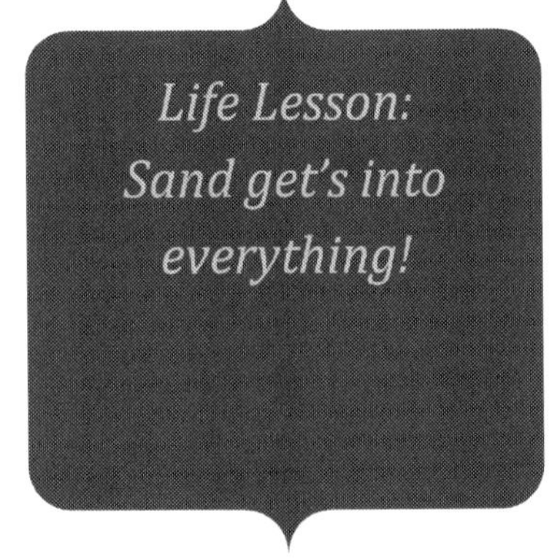

While there are literally hundreds of great stories involving tenants, there are two that stand out in my mind. In the first, a group of young tenants decided to have a huge beach party. They invited all their friends, close acquaintances and neighbors, and picked up all the necessary food, booze and decorations for the event. They also had a truckload of sand delivered.

The sand was spread out across the living room to create an indoor beach. What the young friends didn't realize was that one can't simply vacuum up sand from carpeting, out of ductwork and from every nook and cranny of the house where guests track it. The owner was livid.

The second situation involved a late night phone call from the agency, 'Children and Youth.' I was required to go to a property on Church Street in Allentown, where a tenant had filed a complaint that my firm was allowing children to live in unsafe conditions. Unbeknownst to me, the front door had been kicked in and would not close properly, and therefore anyone could come in and attack or snatch her children in the middle of the night. She wanted something done about my firm's lack of concern for tenants.

Arriving at the property, the representatives of 'Children and Youth' and I found that the tenant was probably stoned. She sat on the sofa with her two kids and yelled at me about her situation. The door had been kicked in by her ex-boyfriend that afternoon, and the tenant claimed that she called my office earlier in the day and had not received any satisfactory repair to the door in the several hours since the door was destroyed. Again, some days it doesn't pay to get out of bed.

Selling with Tenants

Not only can some tenants put our property owners in precarious positions by not paying or by damaging the property, they can also hamper property sales. In one case, we were selling a commercial building that was less than twenty years old, and in fantastic condition, with lots of amenities, a Class A office space. The potential buyer was planning on moving his offices to the second floor, which had been recently vacated, leaving the first floor tenants to continue to occupy the space they had rented for the past ten years.

As we took our final walk through, we discovered a seal had broken on the second floor, causing a small flood in the back two offices on the second floor. Of course, the seller obviously offered to repair the roof immediately, and have the entire area cleaned up, which satisfied the buyer. The tenant on the first floor, however, appeared to be a little shaken, learning that a new owner was taking possession of the building, and immediately began complaining about problems and issues with the property.

Although I had never experienced any difficulty in finding a place to park there, she claimed that there was insufficient parking for the building and that accommodating another business upstairs would exacerbate the problem. Some of her employees had to park as far as two blocks away, she announced. Incidentally, there was a multilevel parking garage across the street, in addition to the large parking lot included with the building.

Secondly, she explained that, since the second floor had been vacant, vagrants had been coming in at night and sleeping there, leaving a mess behind them. However, since the doors locked at five o'clock each evening, I wasn't quite certain how vagrants were getting into the building, if they indeed were. Luckily, despite her claims, the buyer, knowing the value of this particular property, purchased it, but my point is that tenants are so afraid of the possibility of rent increases or the threat of eviction; they make up all sorts of crazy stories in order to avoid change of ownership.

In many situations where we're selling multi-family apartment buildings, the tenants are also concerned that once the new owner takes possession of the property, he will either be evicted or their rent will be raised. What many of them don't understand is that leases stay in place regardless of who the owner is. However, this doesn't seem to stop tenants from being concerned when we show properties, which explains why so many of them make up fantastic stories about the terrible condition of the building.

In one case, I was showing a two unit ranch style apartment building in Heidelberg Township, Pennsylvania which is a rural community surrounded primarily by single family homes. The tenant told my buyer that the structure was infested by roaches and that all efforts to eradicate them had failed.

The tenant went on to say that the roof leaked badly and that, during storms, water poured down in the hallway between the bedrooms, forcing his family to form a bucket brigade.

"It's a very significant roof repair which is going to cost more than ten thousand dollars!" He said.

Seeing that the ceiling in the hallway was dry walled, and noting that there were no water stains whatsoever, no spots, and no nail pops, I asked the tenant to explain just where the water came from, to which, after a bit of dithering, he claimed that it poured through the seams in a way that left no signs of entry, a claim so preposterous that it was all I could do to keep from laughing.

Unfortunately, this is the kind of nonsense that we get pretty regularly from tenants that often scares buyers and investors out of purchasing property. Their reactions are generally based on fear of change.

Forgiveness

Although there are some Amish and Mennonite families still living in my primary market area, most are a bit west of us toward the south central part of Pennsylvania. Some of these rugged and hard-working families have been our clients, and others have helped our team on many occasions by building or repairing horse barns and outbuildings.

By the rolling farmlands of the village of Nickel Mines near Lancaster in October of 2006, a lone gunman entered a one room school house, taking the students hostage and ultimately shooting ten little girls in execution style, killing five of them and permanently disabling others. Marian and Barbie Fisher, 13 and 11, asked that they be shot first, in hopes that others would survive.

The gunman, a milk truck driver who had children of his own, took his own life after shooting the girls, who ranged in age from seven to thirteen years old.

Despite the horror of the gunman's actions and the pain and loss felt by the families of the murdered children, the Amish publically forgave the killer. Members of the Amish community visited and comforted the gunman's widow and parents, even setting up a charitable fund for his family. Amish scholars explained that "letting go of grudges" is part of their culture and belief, as taught by Jesus act of asking that his killers be forgiven.

In their culture, purging any hate of the guilty party or desire for vengeance does not pardon the person responsible for this heinous act, but helps the Amish move toward a better society. They "truly believe that their own forgiveness is bound up in their willingness to forgive others."[xii] Perhaps we all have something to learn from our Amish neighbors.

Chapter 8:
We are a product of our experiences

Although many people believe that genetics make us what we are, and others firmly believe that we are products of our environment, obviously, we are a combination of both. The viewpoints of Gen Xers are vastly different than the viewpoints of Baby Boomers, and the viewpoints of Baby Boomers are very different than those who lived through the Great Depression.

Regardless of whether members of each generation are conservative or liberal, they share some common thoughts and traits because they've experienced the same societal evolution during their lifetimes. For example, when trying to get lists of homes for sale to our clients, we mail listings to seniors and email them to everybody else.

Each person's individual views may be altered by their life experience, whether good or bad. Catastrophic experience of pain or loss can often define people for the remainders of their lives. All of us have some form of regret, some challenges and some personal tragedy in our lives, just as all of us also have memories of great experiences of joy and triumph. The combination of these experiences shape or alter our views.

When we, as salespeople, attempt to entice a prospective client to work with us, we need the prospective client to like and trust us. These two characteristics are the foundation of friendship. In order to build that bond and truly assist our clients, we need to see the world from their perspective and their set of experiences. This doesn't mean that we need to give up our beliefs, and it does not mean that we present a false image of ourselves to our clients, but we need to really understand their beliefs as well.

This same need for us to understand issues from all sides extends to politics, business decisions and even dealing with our own families. Part of my family is made up of highly pro-union blue collar workers and college elites, and another part consists of conservative thinking bankers, engineers and educators. Family reunions are always a whole lot of fun.

My mother grew up in an orphanage in the middle of the coal regions of Pennsylvania. The town is called Pottsville and to this day, there are people living in town that believe the name of the town in the Monkey's song "Clarkesville" is actually Pottsville. They've listened carefully, they say. My mother's family includes coal miners, truck drivers, carpenters and other hard working blue collar individuals. Many of these rugged people came from Ireland, and some of my early memories of her side of the family include echoes of strong Irish accents.

During the early 1940's, my great grandmother became ill with tuberculosis and when my grandmother went to take care of her, they both passed away. None of the extended family had the resources to take on more children, so at the tender age of two, my mother and her older sister were placed into an orphanage with the result that she became closer to her sister than to anyone else in the world.

When, sadly, her sister was killed in her twenties, my mother was left without an immediate family, an experience that affects her outlook to this day. For years, I remember visiting the orphanage with its rows of dormitory beds and the huge walk-in pantry around Christmas. And although I found it exciting, my mother always loathed the place, even though it had been the only home she had ever known as a child.

My earliest memories are of how hard my father worked at several jobs while attempting to complete his doctorate, at times coming home covered from head to toe in black soot from one of his jobs. A treat was chili night when the family split a single bottle of Coke.

Please don't misunderstand me. I did not grow up poor. By the time I was in junior high, my father had completed a doctorate and was an Assistant Superintendent of a moderate sized school district, where we were living in a nice modest three bedroom split level on a quarter acre lot.

By then, I had some understanding of both having and not having. I understood what my family had been able to accomplish through hard work. Hopefully, I've been able to apply that knowledge to positively impact some of those around me.

The Beginning of My Career

In 1990, I stepped off a stage in Philadelphia after receiving an award for being a multimillion dollar producer, one of the top producing agents in the State of Pennsylvania with Century 21. A fellow agent from a competing firm sauntered up to me and snidely asked how, since I was so young, I could possibly have sold so much real estate. At the time, I was twenty-four years old, but I looked

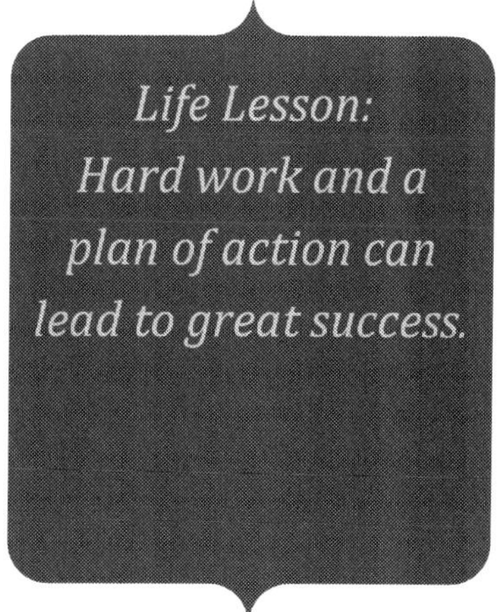

like I was around fifteen.

And although I did not say this, the thought that went through my mind was that I was successful because I had to be. Financially, I was in deep trouble, and I simply had to sell a lot of properties or I would not only go under, but I would take other people who I cared about down with me. As the saying goes, necessity is the mother of invention. I became a top producer because I *had* to become a top producer.

Years later, at a workshop, I met an agent from Florida who told of living in the attic of a barn and mucking out stalls for a living. She started selling real estate part-time in order to earn enough to get a decent apartment. A few years later, she was earning more than a million dollars a year in commissions.

Some of the top real estate agents and brokers that I've had the opportunity to meet with over the years have included people who started their careers while sleeping on someone else's couch, or were the sons and daughters of immigrants, who, despite having no connections or money, became huge successes in the field of real estate.

Desperation is often the linchpin that drives us to those huge successes. I entered the real estate industry in the mid-1980s to help pay my way through college. By 1986 and 1987, the market was skyrocketing in the Northeast, and I started making a very good living by simply sitting around waiting for the phone to ring.

In 1988, my head had swelled up to roughly the size of a watermelon, because I was making more money than any of my friends and, therefore, thought that I was smarter than everybody else.

I talked my father, who at the time was a local school administrator, into buying into the local Century 21 franchise, and then into opening three branch offices in "growth" areas and finally into a land development. After he mortgaged his house to the top of its value, we borrowed even more money at high interest rates. But I wasn't worried, because I could always make more money, right?

1988, however, was the year of the great real estate crash in the Northeast. Property sales didn't simply slow down, they virtually stopped. My father had been looking forward to retirement, and we now owed nearly a million and a half with no substantial income to pay the payments. Now, in 1988, a million and a half was such a huge sum of money that he was in risk of losing his home, and all because of the fact that I had bought into the irrational exuberance of the real estate market at that time.

I was not someone who ever wanted to call a total stranger or knock on someone's door, but I also knew that I had to do whatever it took to find buyers and sellers. My father juggled numbers and credit, and I started calling people who were trying to sell their homes "for sale by owner," "farming" neighborhoods and sleeping very little. I wasn't really taking home much money because I was working simply to pay that huge debt.

Ultimately, we survived. In fact, we came through the several year downturn in the market like a sling shot. At the time, however, I didn't think there'd be a day after tomorrow for me, at least financially.

What really helped to save us, while many of our competitors closed their doors, was finding ways to capture a larger share of the real estate market and create business. The truth is, as I have said before, that sales are always being negotiated in any market, good or bad. Some need to buy or sell because of job relocation needs. Others may have leases ending, a baby on the way, a pending divorce, a death in the family, or any number of reasons. My challenge was to identify those people who truly want or need to move.

We survived and I became stronger for that experience. Humans, like all animals, have always grown and developed through survival of the fittest. We learn, adapt and grow. I am *not* suggesting that we throw away part of our population, but rather that we rise to the occasion when faced with adversity and we adapt.

Part of the problem we have with society today is that we have an entitlement mentality. We *expect* someone to take care of us, so we don't have the same strong incentives to be the best that we can be. Certainly, we need the safety net of unemployment compensation, welfare and insurance programs, but have we gone too far? I know this statement is not politically correct in the current environment, but the problem with our all inclusive safety net is that there's no real incentive to work. Why clean toilets or pick up trash in order to provide for your family when you can earn more sitting on unemployment? Desperation is what pushes us to be the best we can be rather than live in complacency.

In my opinion, those who believe that we exist as a collective and that it is our mutual responsibility to take care of each other are somewhat misguided. On the surface, that sounds great, but the truth is that there is no incentive for individuals to rise up and better themselves, creating new products and services, if there is no benefit for their hard work.

I think it's a great idea to try to help people find jobs. I think it's admirable to contribute to the poor, and help the starving people of the world. I am not taking issue with that. What I have a problem with is that far too many individuals and families have become dependent on the system, and the system, my friends, is you and me. One of the greatest fallacies in our society is that we believe the government has the power and money to fix problems. The government has no money of its own. The government gets the money to do its work by confiscating it from us in taxes or by printing it, which, because we're in a world economy, devalues the dollar around the globe and forces us to be able to buy less goods and services.

The system that was supposed to be a government for the people and by the people has been fundamentally altered to a new system in which we are forced to give away more than half of what we earn in the form of income taxes, social security taxes, property taxes, school taxes, sales taxes and other taxes to the government with the result that it is often spent to no advantage, by which I mean that in too many cases, these government agencies take money from us, and give it to other groups who chose not to work, who chose to live a lifestyle where they don't have to make the hard choices. This, for me at least, constitutes a problem.

In The Declaration of Independence, our founding fathers wrote that, "all men are created equal," which does not mean that all men should receive equally from the government, but rather that we all have equal opportunity and equal freedom. Thomas Jefferson wrote "The policy of the American government is to leave their citizens free, neither restraining nor aiding them in their pursuits."[xiii] He also wrote, "The democracy will cease to exist when you take away from those who are willing to work and give to those who would not." [xiv] Today, nearly fifty percent of Americans pay no federal income tax, and yet government programs continue to expand and grow, offering more programs to those who vote politicians into office.

Again, yes there are people in need, but there are also people living on the government dole that do not need to be, all in the interest of the nanny state and "fairness." Part of the reason that communism completely failed in so many parts of the world is because those countries took away their citizen's incentives. If everyone is equal and if everyone receives the same share of food, of shelter, of clothing, and of money as everybody else, then what incentive is there to work and try to rise above everyone else? What incentive is there to work hard and create?

Further, if we become that collective that we're moving toward, looking to government for all that we have and being ruled by a central planning or governing body, will we ever invent again? Would someone in China have invented the computer, the television or the iPod if the inventor had to go to the government and make the proposal to a bureaucrat?

One of the reasons that many historians believe the Soviet Union went through periods of food shortages and actual starvation was that individuals stopped working for the benefit of others. If the person next to you isn't working very hard, or is regularly absent from work, and you're carrying his load and you earn the same wages at the end of the day, eventually you'll stop working so hard as well.

Let's look at it the other way. There's a great incentive not to work at all, because you get money, and shelter, and food, regardless of what you do or don't do. We are, sadly moving in a direction of taking care of people who really don't try to take care of themselves. The greatest success stories in our country are about people who rose up above adversity, and made something of themselves.

There are people who, instead of waiting around for something to happen, accepted a great challenge in their life. They may have failed once or twice or many times before they found a way to succeed. Abraham Lincoln failed repeatedly until he was elected president and helped to end slavery.

Our society screams about the excesses and profits of the rich, but really, who have been the wealthiest individuals of the last few decades? Sam Walton who owned Walmart came from nothing and built the world's most successful department stores. Bill Gates never graduated from college. The creators of Google certainly didn't come from rich families. Steve Jobs of Apple Computer, Michael Dell of Dell Computer, Mary Kay, Stephen Spielberg and so many others came from modest backgrounds. Simon Cowell was a mailroom employee in a music publishing company. Even a hundred years ago, Henry Ford was a simple machinist with a dream and Walt Disney built an empire from his imagination. Strong desire, hard work, and innovation took these people to the top of their fields. Did they deserve their success? Were the invention of the iPod and the creation of Disneyworld worth these individuals amassing great wealth?

We have to look to these people, and realize that we're creating a society that is antithetical to the growth and success of our country and our way of life. Unfortunately, I could never run for political office, because someone would take these words, and turn them around to make it sound like I hate the poor or I hate the downtrodden. That's not the case at all. It's the old story of teaching someone to fish rather than giving someone a fish, teaching someone to fish so that they can take care of themselves.

I believe in people, I believe in the human spirit. I believe that most people, left to their own devices, will find a way not only to simply survive, but to succeed. I believe most people don't need to be taken care of.   I believe that most people really can do great things when they're put in a position where they have to. So let's help those who truly need help which, unfortunately is only about one out of every fifty citizens to whom the government sends checks. And by the way, don't forget that this is *our* money they're sending.

One other quick thought on the subject of success. We need to spend more time thinking of what's possible and less time complaining about all the bad things that have happened to us, or imagining that society is unfair.

Dr. Denis Waitley, the author of such best-selling books as *The Seeds of Greatness* and *The Psychology of Winning* stresses that we tend to move toward what we think about most. Just as the promise of a limitless income and a great lifestyle has brought immigrants to

America, the same lure appeals to those entering the field of real estate.

The reason that so many immigrants become great successes with little or no money when they arrive in the country, while so many natural born Americans fail to reach their goals is the strength of their conviction that if you believe you can, you can. If you believe that society is unfair and life is stacked against you, you will fail. Think of all those successful individuals outlined earlier.

I really believe this is one of the primary reasons those who win the Powerball tend to lose it all very quickly. Their subconscious tells them that they shouldn't have the money, they're not worthy and they will lose it, and in fact, they do. Focus on the positive. Be conscious of pitfalls, but focus on what's possible and move toward your goals.

Pain, Regret and Loss

As I mentioned earlier in this chapter, everyone has some source of pain in their life. Some of the pain we experience is the result of injury, disease, or the loss of those close to us, whether as a result of something like death or divorce. The purchase and sale of homes is often directly related to these painful experiences.

Life Lesson: Live every moment as if it's your last. Find whatever joy you can in the present.

As I work with the challenges of others, I am thankful every day for the life I've had. Of course, there have been significant struggles and disappointments, but I've also experienced some great opportunities, happiness and accomplishment. Ironically enough, according to today's standards, I was raised in a dysfunctional family since my father and mother never got divorced, my father worked hard for everything we had, and my mother stayed home.

My first introduction to tragedy occurred when I was a young child. A family in our neighborhood was waiting for their father to come home on Christmas Eve when the police came to their house to tell them that he had been killed in an automobile accident. Since then I have always been aware of how short life can be, and that we never know from one moment to the next when tragedy will strike.

When listing homes for sale, many of our clients tell us their own stories of personal tragedy that define their lives. Those who served as soldiers during wartime may tell us that moment when half their platoon was killed and they somehow miraculously survived. Other clients tell us of the loss of a spouse or a child. I was particularly haunted by clients who had to sell their home because, following the suicide of their son, they could no longer bear to live there.

The pain this couple suffered is something I pray every day I never have to experience. We've had a number of these situations over the years. The saddest part of the story was that after they moved, their remaining son suffered an allergic reaction and also passed away suddenly. What I personally took away from this is that we have to treat each moment with our family as a blessing because life can be short and unkind.

The Winter Scare

Although I have been in plenty of accidents, been shot at, and even attacked, the closest my family has come to personal tragedy happened in our back yard. We have a couple of acres in a beautiful neighborhood adjacent to a game preserve. Our yard gently slopes back a few hundred feet to a level area and then drops sixty feet or so into deep valley between our home and the neighbors behind.

Two winters ago, a sudden freeze created a sheer coat of ice on the top of the packed snow in my yard. It was bitter cold and getting dark, but my children wanted to sled in the yard and my wife acquiesced, instructing them to be careful. Ordinarily, they would sled down the gentle slope from our side yard to the back, coming to a stop along the level part of the yard.

As Theresa watched our four year old from the window, Kourtney's sled failed to stop and pitched over the crest of the yard into the trees beyond. Fearing she had fallen sixty feet through the trees, my wife rushed out the door wearing only a t-shirt and jeans. Theresa and the other kids ran to the back of the property, only to encounter the same solid ice, causing all of them to lose their footing, fall and slide down the hill behind my youngest daughter.

None were injured, but they were trapped, unable to get back up the hill of solid ice, with a wind chill of near zero and no way to get help. After more than an hour of effort, my oldest daughter was able to climb out and phone for assistance. Although Bridgett tried sliding warm clothing and a coat back down the hill to my wife, they didn't reach her.

By the time I pulled in my driveway, the fire department was extracting them with rope tied to stakes hammered down the back of the yard. Despite the fact that they were only two hundred feet from our home, it took a full complement of rescue workers to pull them out. The power of weather can be frighteningly awesome, as anyone who has witnessed a tornado or major hurricane may attest.

> *Life Lesson:*
> *Be careful, be vigilant... and always carry a cell phone!*

Astonishingly, Theresa had very little frostbite, although she was bright red and, when placed on a dining room chair, shook so violently that the entire chair bounced up and down. Since the kids all had coats, they were in better shape.

Life can be unpredictable. Be thankful for each day you're given in this life!

The British Author

One of the most frustrating challenges of selling real estate is that our clients are often at such emotional peaks that they are aggressive, angry or both. But we can learn from this, and in so doing better understand our own lives.

Even generally, watching people's reactions can be fun and interesting. For example, I was sitting at a table with four other authors signing books in Orlando, Florida in the fall of 2008 after the release of my book *How to Sell Your Home in Any Market*.

This particular book signing was sponsored by the National Association of Realtors so most of those in the audiences had been real estate agents and brokers, mortgage brokers or sales people. Most people simply asked us to autograph their copy of the book and stayed to chat a bit. It was a very relaxed atmosphere until another author joined us. This particular author was a tall, good looking, silver-haired gentleman, probably in his early fifties, and surrounded by women ranging from their twenties to much, much older. And each, when it came her turn to have her copy signed, managed to touch him on the hand or wrist.

Life Lesson: Be honest and true with yourself.

Later, when I pointed this out to him, he admitted that it often happened, why he did not know. Perhaps, he suggested, it was his British accent, but I think there was more to it myself.

Every single woman did it, and I found that intriguing since no other customer had touched any other author in the room, and I've wondered ever since whether the sheer attractiveness is what leads people to need that physical touch or whether there's some other draw that creates the need for someone to physically touch someone else.

I honestly believe if a female author had been sitting in the same chair, and men came up and grasped her hand, one after another she would probably feel threatened, yet the reverse was both pleasurable to the man and seemed to be a physical need of the women as they spoke with him.

Meeting the In-Laws

On another occasion, I was meeting much of my wife's family for the first time at a birthday party for my wife's uncle. They are a very Pennsylvania Dutch crowd, which in most areas would be called "German," but for some reason, in Pennsylvania, are known as "Dutch." One interesting characteristic of my wife's family and of many Pennsylvania Dutch families I've encountered is that they appear to be able to handle heavy amounts of liquor without even feeling it. The gentlemen at the birthday party, including some of Theresa's cousins

Life Lesson:
Be careful what you do in front of family. They will be part of your life forever!

and uncles, were all drinking shots of something they call Goldschläger. I asked what it was and they explained that it was a form of peppermint schnapps.

Now, I've had peach schnapps in the past, and since that is not a very strong liquor, I felt fairly safe drinking these shots with the guys. I actually thought drinking this obscene burning substance might help me to fit in better with her family. It turns out that Goldschläger is more than one hundred proof. After six shots they decided to have a little fun with me by pouring half glasses.

After the first half glass, I'm told that I wandered around, embarrassing myself quite severely in front of most of the family that I was meeting for the first time, from babbling incessantly to doing something or other with a broom.

What can I say? You have to be very careful around the Dutch!

College Pranks

One of my best friends in high school and college was David Zinczenko, who is now world-famous because of his magazine *Men's Health*, and his books, the *Abs Diet*, and *Eat This, Not That*. Although I haven't see much of him over the past few years, whenever I do, I am reminded of how entertaining he could be, primarily because of the outrageous stunts he liked to pull.

Life Lesson: Remember to set aside time for a little fun in life.

In school I was always trying to get a laugh by pulling pranks of which some of *my* best included releasing a live pigeon in the middle of the cafeteria during a lunch period in which chicken was on the menu, as well as attending lunch wearing an exterminator's outfit, complete with gas mask, and nailing up a condemned sign next to the checkout register, a performance that got me sent up to the principal's office. Perhaps because my father was Assistant Superintendent of the next school district over, I didn't get expelled. Although there might have been another reason, as I remember that Mr. Kline was laughing when I was ushered in.

"Loren," he said, "if you keep up these pranks, you are going to give me a heart attack, I'm going to die and you're going to feel badly. Would that be a good thing?"

Anyway, David did things like playing bumper cars on Route 22, a four lane divided highway. I'd be driving along and feel a thud in the back as he bumped into me with no warning. Of course, those were in the days when car bumpers were actually made out of metal, not whatever form of plastic they appear to be comprised of today.

And then there was John, the kind of guy who would serve mixed drinks at a party, and put a little bit of liquid nitrogen into them so that smoke would roll all over the counter top. John made a bet with David that he could drive a car blindfolded down 4th Street in South Bethlehem, a bet that, for some unknown reason, David took him up on with the result that he sat, terrified as John, blindfolded as promised, sped for a block or so along 4th Street. I expect that the impressions from his fingerprints are still on the seat cushion.

Neil and his Date

While discussing pranks, I'd like to share a quick story about Neil, an old friend of mine. My friends and I knew that Neil had been dating a girl in North Bethlehem and that they frequently parked in a lot behind her home. Planning to prank them on one particular Friday night, we prepared for our mission by stopping at a grocery store to pick up about eight rolls of toilet paper, two tubes of toothpaste, and other assorted items.

When we spotted his car, we turned out our headlights, and rolled down to park behind him, delighted to see that his windows were so steamed up that we were able to completely cover the car with toilet paper and coat the door handles with toothpaste without his being aware that anyone was around.

After that, we drove to his house, parked out front and waited the forty-five minutes that it took him to show up. He was, needless to say, in a highly agitated state. In fact, as soon as he saw us, he shouted, "Just get in range of my fist!" I turned to my friend Todd in the passenger seat to find he was no longer sitting there. Looking back, Todd was standing next to Neil offering him his chin.

Luckily Neil broke down in laughter. It was one of our best toilet papering jobs ever.

My Cousin Kyle

In the heyday of downtown Allentown, there was a huge department store called Hess's on Hamilton Street, right in the center of the city. The owner, Max Hess, was a unique businessman and the object of many stories around town, living in a huge mansion with a full nightclub in the lower level. Max had created a string of large department stores, very similar to Macys, but none were as grand as this gorgeous downtown jewel, complete with soaring ceilings, gaudy chandeliers and even a mezzanine.

On the lower level of the building, Hess's famous Patio Restaurant featured enormous portions and decadent desserts, as well as a steady stream of models, displaying the latest Hess fashions.

And there were escalators, a novelty in those days, packed with patrons and their packages. On one such busy day, many years ago, during a visit to the store, my Aunt Adrienne and her young son Kyle were shopping close to the escalator which, to the consternation of the shoppers on it, suddenly came to a halt, pitching people forward. Only later was it discovered that Kyle, ingenious as always when it came to machinery, had managed to immobilize the escalator by pushing his pinkie into a keyhole at the bottom. Adrienne was mortified.

Even as a child, Kyle was the one family member that everyone talked about, and not just because of the fact that he could shut down an entire escalator system. The escalator wasn't his only exceptional feat. When he was five, he pulled a bank vault door shut, locking his mother and a bank teller inside. His mother and the teller were released unharmed but visibly shaken.

That same year, he entertained everyone at a family gathering by showing that he could create a stream and waterfall on the staircase. His mother was not pleased, but it was certainly funny and I'm pretty sure that at another family function, he swallowed a goldfish.

One of my favorite "Kyle Stories" occurred when he was around twenty and he and his friends were on a scavenger hunt somewhere in Georgia where he was attending school. One of the items on the list was to get the largest sign possible and bring it back. Armed with a battery operated drill and a ladder, he proceeded to the front of the County Sheriff's office and he unscrewed one side of the sign, causing it to flip over.

Before he could get to the second side, a deputy's car pulled up in front of the office. "What are you boy's doing?" He asked.

"I'm waiting for the late bus," Kyle said, holding the drill behind him and not missing a beat. The deputy pulled away without noticing the dangling sign above them.

Each of us, being unique, touches those around us in different ways. My cousin Kyle was only in his thirties when he passed away this year while visiting Disney World with his step daughter. He had been seriously injured on the set of the movie *Transformers 2* and had never quite recovered. He was truly a unique person.

Kyle, you will be missed.

Chapter 9:
Struggling with Outside Forces

America was founded on individual freedom. We had the rights to succeed or fail based on our own efforts and not to be ruled by a king as we were when we were first colonized. Sadly, history repeats itself. Over the past fifty or sixty years, agencies have developed their own fiefdoms of power in both the local communities and the country at large.

On an almost daily basis, the real estate community has to navigate the waters of legal paperwork and government agencies in order to assist clients. Zoning boards, planning commissions, environmental protection and politicians all figure into real estate development and the new rules of using your own property.

Municipalities and Government Agencies

I struggle frequently to deal with government agencies that oversee different aspects of our business and our industry, and I am challenged, at times, to deal with politicians and offices that hold control over zoning. Some of them are very easy to deal with and are wonderful people just trying to protect their area. Others, however, are overzealous and want very badly to control the development of anything that happens in their area, and, of course, some of them simply allow power to go to their heads.

Rules usually start with good intentions. A township doesn't want the property values to decline, so they pass a regulation that requires homeowners to maintain the exteriors, keeping up with painting and the lawn. Then the rules might be taken a little further by some who believe that all homes in a particular area should be painted with complimentary colors and have flowers in front, or rear yard fences should be outlawed because they hurt the natural view from the backyards, pools should be restricted because some feel they look "ugly" and regulations and restrictions mount.

In writing this section, I should be careful what I say because I'm slightly concerned that I'll be getting registered letters from townships all across Pennsylvania telling me that some application somewhere is denied for no particular reason. As you might understand, my firm represents land owners who wish to sell land for development and we also assist clients who want to change the way in which they make use of their property, both of which require approvals from their local municipalities.

Additionally, we sell small businesses, like Subway restaurants, Curves, laundry mats, gas stations, and so on. These are known as business opportunities. When we market and sell business opportunities, we have to deal with various different government agencies.

In one case we were in the process of selling a hair salon, only to discover that there are regulations governing the equipment which must be available. In the process of one of these sales, an inspector arrived to make certain that the salon had the proper number of towels and the correct implements, including a precise number of brand new combs.

The owner of the salon pulled out four boxes of combs, each containing one hundred combs, along with a handful of loose combs. "There you go," she said. "We have plenty."

"I'm supposed to watch you count them," he replied.

I thought he was kidding. He wasn't. Looking back, I still wonder if he was simply trying to fulfill his role as a ball buster, or if he wanted one last opportunity to look down her low cut blouse. Whatever the case, she had the guts to register a protest.

"I certainly have more than enough," she told him. "I have over four hundred."

"My report has to specify exactly how many combs you have," he explained. "I need to watch you count them."

And so, while customers waited, our salon owner had to sit and count out combs for this government official.

Rules, regulations and laws are created to protect the public. Perhaps there is a rule that requires a hairdresser to have sufficient combs that she does not use the same comb on two customers, but too many of our regulations have lost the spirit of the requirement in lieu of subjugation by each agency.

The Assisted Living Facility...

In another case, involving an assisted living facility which, like most others, was designed in such a way as to provide a staff to provide assistance to those who can, on the whole, live independent lives, we ran into unexpected trouble.

Before the property could be sold, we had to go through a series of inspections, one of which lasted seven hours and culminated in the citation of a violation.

Apparently, all waste paper baskets in assisted living facilities must be covered.   I'm certain that there are substantial reasons behind why waste paper baskets have to be closed, but if I happened to be a sixty-five year old individual living in a small condo, and I have an open waste paper basket next to my desk, and I choose to move into an apartment in an assisted living facility, and I bring with me my waste paper basket, I didn't realize I would be breaking some great Pennsylvania law. You might as well get out the handcuffs now.

This particular inspector went into nothing short of a tirade about how rules are rules, and they must be followed, and we need to be more conscious of what is required in an assisted living facility. This was my first experience with the agency that oversees these facilities. A few short weeks later I, unfortunately, had my second experience with state government officials at an assisted living facility.

The Second Assisted Living Facility

Despite the fact than an eighty bed facility just outside Lancaster, Pennsylvania, sported modern elevators, a beauty salon, full restaurant kitchen, dining hall and a family room complete with fireplace, the inspector presented us with seven pages of violations, including one which stated that the residents' rooms were too small.

When I suggested that a change could be made which would provide for single rather than double room occupancy, I was told that the facility license would be revoked and the facility closed. There was no room for discussion.

And when I expressed interest in turning the building into an apartment complex, he explained that a zoning variance had been issued to allow for an assisted living facility, period. Furthermore, since the building's height exceeded that presently permitted, it was his belief that this multimillion dollar building would have to be razed because it did not meet present requirements.

"So if some paper pusher in the state decides a thirty or forty year old building isn't good enough for our seniors, it should immediately be torn down?" I told him. "Is that really what you're telling me?"

The state official ignored me, explaining that many buildings across the state were not up to standards, and it was his job to shut down any that did not meet current requirements which meant, he added proudly, that his department expected to close about a third of all facilities in the state.

I asked him why the government would consider shutting down these homes when there was such a need for them with the population aging. Where would the baby boomers spend their final golden years if facilities specifically built for them were closed? I demanded.

Now it was his turn to become agitated.

We argued back and forth for some time, because this made absolutely no sense to me at all. We were talking about a beautiful, well equipped building designed to meet every need of the seniors who were currently living there. Besides, what was supposed to happen to them? But all he kept saying was, "These conditions the residents are being forced to live in…"

"Some of these people have been living here for as long as a decade," I protested. "This is the only home that they've known for the last ten years. I wouldn't be surprised if relocation might not mean that a good many of them would die."

In the end, he threw the papers at me and left, but ultimately it was a shallow victory because he was successful in closing the facility. All of which is one more example of an unfortunate fact of life. Government officials are always right and everyone else is absolutely wrong. Whenever government is involved, there seems to be no middle ground.

Zoning Officials and Building Inspectors

We run into similar problems with zoning officers on a regular basis. In some cases people get elected to zoning boards simply to alter the makeup of an area, changing it into what they perceive it should be. Obviously I make money from the development of land into housing projects, shopping centers, stores, and so on.

However I, like everyone else, love to look out over beautiful farmland, spacious park systems, and unobstructed hills and valleys. But I'm also a pragmatist. I sell a lot of farms and I know that the family farm in Eastern Pennsylvania and the surrounding states has become very difficult to maintain for many reasons, including that it's expensive to hire workers to work the farm profitably.

The amount of money that farmers are able to obtain from selling crops is not great, even in the best of times, and taxes continue to go higher and higher on both land and income. Eventually, many farmers sell their property off to developers or develop parts of their land in order to have enough money to continue doing what they love to do, or in order to retire without having to face living in abject poverty after years of long hours tilling the soil. In some areas we've run across zoning boards that have passed laws restricting the use of the farm. The basic concept behind a 90-10 law, for example, is that a farmer is forbidden, through the zoning laws, from significantly subdividing their farms.

Let me explain it another way. Pennsylvania laws, much like other states, require that every township must set aside a certain percentage of its land for multi-family housing, such as apartments, condos and town houses, as well as for industrial and commercial land, and for single family houses. However, these regulations can be skirted. For example, a one hundred acre parcel of land may be zoned for one house per acre with the result that a development of seventy or eighty houses could be built there, making allowance for open spaces and roads.

Under a 90-10 law, a farmer may only develop ten percent of his total acreage which in turn means that if he has a one hundred acre farm, he can only put houses on ten percent of it or ten acres, meaning he may get away with putting seven or eight houses on a corner somewhere, and the rest of the land has to be preserved as a farm. There are many different variations of these rules such as 70-30 rules that preserve the farm for only a certain period of time, while under other regulations, farms may be preserved forever.

The problem is that zoning practices which restrict property use significantly devalue the land. A builder may be willing to pay fifteen to twenty five thousand dollars per acre for land that they can develop into lots in the current marketplace. Land in the same area that is restricted to a farm use can only be sold somewhere in the neighborhood of three to six thousand dollars per acre, because there is only so much money that can be made from planting crops or raising cattle. This zoning struggle often appears to occur when individuals or families move to a rural location from an urban location, such as New York or Philadelphia, buy a half acre or one acre parcel overlooking someone else's farm and fall in love with the view.

These new residents then run for election to a zoning board, and convince people that it's a great idea to restrict the use of land because, after all, don't we want to keep space open for our future generations? In theory this sounds like a great idea, but in practice, struggling farmers who had always, in the past, been able to sub-divide part of the land and use it for housing, are significantly hurt by the devaluing of the land by restricting the use to which it can be put. This is another example of what often happens when the collective is favored at the expense of hard working individuals who have spent years tilling the soil.

A few years ago, I engaged in an argument with a member of a zoning board who explained to me that when the particular farmer that we were discussing had purchased the farm, it had been for the express purpose of growing potatoes and not converting into a housing development, equating it to buying a pizza place, and then trying to sell a liquor store.

"They are two different things," he explained. "He bought a farm. He can sell a farm. He didn't buy a housing development. He doesn't own a housing development, and he certainly doesn't have any right to sell a housing development."

I explained that when the farmer purchased his land, he was investing in a property that had far more uses a few years ago than it does today based on the restrictions that were put on that land. I don't have an answer to the problem of open space, but I'm vehemently opposed to taking away peoples' rights to do with their property what they choose to do with it.

In 1772, Samuel Adams wrote "What liberty can there be where property is taken away without consent?"[xv] Our ability to own our own property and utilize that property in any way we like is one of the greatest freedoms our country offers. If society wants to maintain open spaces, they should collectively purchase it. Many of our original park systems came into being by way of money donated not only by the rich but by groups of people interested in protecting the environment against development. Admirably, they invested in society's future, but remember that it was their *choice* to do so. It was not forced upon them.

In far too many instances, government has been used as a way to simply take from one group and give to another. In this case, using legislation, they are taking value away from one family and giving a view to another. I prefer not to see government simply take away peoples' rights, devaluing property in order to benefit someone else. It's simply not right. This is supposed to be a free society, and as Ralph Williams, who was a mentor of mine, used to say, "Land ownership and the use of that land is a tip of the iceberg of free society. If you can't own land, and use that land you can't truly be free."

Attorney Posturing

Two years ago, an attorney called me out of the blue to inform me that a courier was en route to my office to pick up a file dealing with a transaction that one of our agents settled the prior year. When he specified that he wanted the original file, I protested with the result that he said that if I wanted to grill him, he could have a subpoena drawn up within a half an hour. The Sheriff, he assured me, would serve papers on me by the afternoon and then he'd find a way to file contempt charges.

"I'm not trying to be argumentative," I told him, "but I know the state requires us to keep all files in the office. They are not allowed to leave under the law."

When he said the file belongs to the client, and therefore, has the right to have it, I explained, knowing that that was not the case, that although there was paperwork in the file that certainly did belong to the client, our agency was entitled to copies of that paperwork, and there was also paperwork in most files that did not belong to the client, including forms and accounting ledgers that are our in-house information, and is not information the client needs, or is entitled to see.

"I'd really like to know what this is in reference to," I added.

His answer, delivered at the top of his voice, was that he was not going to put up with my insolence, and that a subpoena would be issued immediately.

"I'll be seeing you in court," he concluded.

Before he could hang up I told him that he couldn't sue me because the senior partner in his law firm had once represented me. Without full disclosure and written permission by both parties, law firms are precluded from representing both parties in a potential law suit.

At that point he became flustered and calmed down. The large fee he planned to make from going after a large real estate broker was dwindling away, and he said that his concern was that one of our clients had overpaid for a house, and he believed the client was discriminated against.

All this transpired in 2006 at the very peak of the real estate market when houses in our area were selling in just hours or days, and many, many sales were the result of multiple bids. Buyers were so desperate to buy homes that they often bid over the asking price.

When he told me that he understood that three bids had been made on a particular property, and that the seller had accepted his client's bid, I said, "That's great. Then what seems to be the problem?"

Life Lesson:
Be aware that we're
all interconnected.

His explanation amazed me. It seems that his client, convinced that our brokerage house made a habit of gouging protected ethnic classes, in order to bid successfully for the property, believed he had to offer more than the asking price. Obviously, that's ludicrous.

Many homes in a hot market sell for over full price, and we really don't care whether the buyer is pink, black, green, purple, polka-dotted or striped. In fact, many of our agents are pink, black, green and purple, although we have yet to hire one that's either poke dotted or striped. Our goal is to represent a client to the best of our ability, which means that we do our best to facilitate their purchase of the property they want to own.

Every client is given the opportunity for legal representation. Every client is given the opportunity to bid what they want. We also give people the facts of life. If the market is very slow a buyer may want to start with a lower offer, and try and get the property for as little as possible. In a very hot market where we're representing a buyer, if the buyer truly wants the house he may have to pay full price, and in a multi-bid situation he may have to pay over full price.

Needless to say, I never heard from the attorney again.

Politics and Power

Government agencies, and to a lesser extent, attorneys, whether they're local, state or national, use the tax and legal system to keep our population in check in a way that was never intended by the founding fathers of our country. For example, in the fall of 2008 I heard from the Executive Director of the Home Builders Association in the Dayton Beach area in Florida who informed me that the Home Builders Association was planning to sue their county because of the excessive fees they were being charged just for the privilege of building a home for a client near that area. She said something called a school impact fee was going up from six thousand dollars to over eight thousand five hundred, and that the total impact fees between different government agencies that charged the builder for the privilege of building a property were going up to nearly twenty five thousand dollars per house.

Life Lesson: Freedom can be taken away if we're not vigilant.

This fee is excessive in that a builder may be building a town home in the area that'll sell for $170,000 or $180,000. The builder will be making somewhere between an eight and a fifteen percent profit margin on the construction of the house, in this case somewhere between $13,000 and $27,000. The local government is taking the same or more than the builder will take in profit for all of the builder's hard work. Keep in mind that, after the builder builds the house, and takes that small profit margin, the builder will then have to pay local, state, and federal income taxes. In order to pay these fees, builders have to raise their prices, which may make them unaffordable.

In 2008, the Florida real estate market had crashed through the floor, which meant that some government agencies were receiving less money in taxes. The difference, however, between the private sector, in this case the builders, and the local government is that in order for the builders to keep their homes and feed their families, they have to work harder, reduce their margins, and do whatever it takes to try and scrape some money together by selling houses, building additions, or whatever else it takes. If, on the other hand, the government loses a little bit of income, they simply raise the taxes on you and me to make up for what they feel is a shortfall, or create new taxes and hide them.

In this particular case in Florida, the school district and county ultimately acquiesced because the increased fees truly hurt the affordability of homes in the area.[xvi]

I've met a number of politicians that honestly feel that it is only due to their largess that we are allowed to keep even part of the money we have earned, an attitude that can be illustrated by an argument to which I was privy between my former broker, Bill Huber and a local municipal government agency of which he had been a board member.

Bill had argued that this municipal agency had been successfully billing about 2,400 customers for several years with one part time employee, and when faced with a growth rate of only a few hundred customers, the agency had found it necessary not only to hire several employees but to enlarge their office space, and that all of this had been paid for by raising the cost of the municipal service that was a necessity in the area.

Bill's argument was that, although the impact on the general consumer was not significantly higher, there was no real need to grow that agency, that the agency was just creating its own fiefdom or pyramid of power, and growing itself for the sake of growth. Even if the impact to the individual resident wasn't very high, the unnecessary growth of dozens of these small parts of government add up and take away more of our resident's disposable income.

A Warrant for My Arrest!

One of my real estate offices is located in a suburban township in Pennsylvania, which taxes us in a variety of ways. One of those taxes is called a "business privilege tax" and we receive it by mail. Recently, having received two copies of a bill, I paid one in the mistaken assumption that I simply received the same bill twice. In reality, they were billing twice, once as a company, and once as an independent contractor because, although I am President of the company, a requirement placed on real estate agencies in the state is that all licensees are independently employed as an independent contractors.

This was not made clear to me until, on an early mid-afternoon in October, when, my wife having gone into labor with our fourth child, I was met by the sheriff who was serving a warrant for my arrest based on my failure to pay a fifteen dollar business privilege tax on myself. While my father, who happened to be visiting me at the time, argued with the sheriff, I went to be at my wife's side during the delivery of my daughter, after which I went directly to the District Justice's office, and told them I'd be happy to pay the fine. Incidentally, the fine for not paying the fifteen dollar tax was three hundred dollars. This is more than Big Vinnie gets for loaning you money on a gambling debt.

It took a while before one of the two receptionists, both of whom appeared to be engaged in a game of solitaire on the computer, noticed me standing at the window of the District Justice's office.

I explained that I had to pay this fine, and I told her I was a little offended that I didn't receive a phone call or a registered letter telling me that I was fifteen dollars in default. For one thing, it would have avoided an outrageous penalty for a small fee, and for another thing, I saw no reason why an arrest warrant should be issued. Had circumstances been different, would the sheriff have shown up at my office to put me in handcuffs?

"What has happened to this country? " I demanded.

She responded to me, and I quote, "Everyone has to pay their fair share."

"Why? Is it so we can hire a third or fourth receptionist to play solitaire?" I responded.

She was highly offended by my words, but let me be honest. Early in the history of the United States, Debtor's prisons were outlawed. There are people who have owed me money that I will never be able to collect, but I don't have the power of law enforcement behind me to go and simply arrest them. I think it's a wrong practice, and I think these government agencies are simply taking far too much power for themselves. The taking of our individual freedoms in return for security has been an incremental process.

For example, the government has created Social Security to take care of the nation's elderly. And then, instead of putting that money away for us, they put it into a general fund. Then congress takes that general fund and spends that money on things that were never meant to be part of our system and in so doing, uses up our money and requires the government to charge us even more. But the government claims it's all for our benefit.

As an aside, the former chairman of the NASDAQ stock exchange Bernie Madoff talked clients into investing through his wealth management firm and used each new investment to pay dividends to prior investors, creating a house of cards because there was no true investment. Madoff was arrested, of course, because in business, this is an illegal practice known as a Ponzi scheme and is illegal. In government, we call the same practice 'Social Security.'

Wow! And we keep electing these people.

The Story of Mr. M

Mr. M was the rumored owner of approximately two thousand homes, apartment buildings and parcels of land in Pennsylvania when I was asked to meet with him in regard to the valuation of these properties in the early 1990's. I had seen articles in the newspaper in which Mr. M had been dubbed a "Slum Lord", and there were even editorials expounding on the terrible conditions in which he "forced" so many people to live.

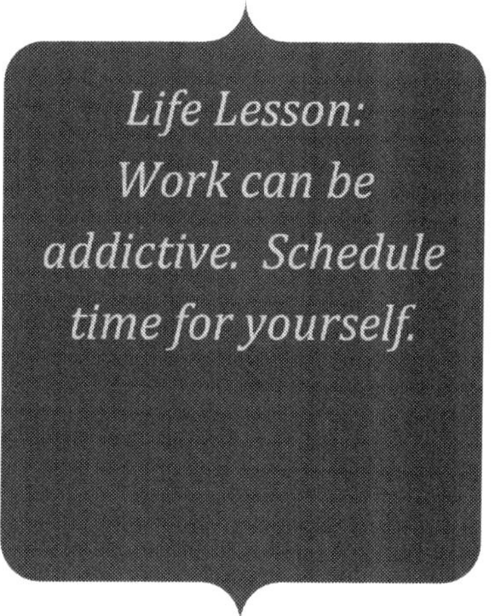

In fact, his apartment buildings and tenements were said to be in such squalid and poor condition, that living there was akin to living in Beirut. Based on the media coverage, my expectations werc that I was about to meet one of the least desirable people of my career. I imagined a greasy, slimy man with slicked back hair, rubbing his hands together in anticipation of the next day rent would be due.

His office was in Easton, Pennsylvania, and I noticed that he had no mailbox. There were no numbers on the door, his windows were blacked out, and his mail slot through his front door was sealed shut. I later learned that this was a technique to avoid being served with documentation from a court.

I knocked loudly on the door several times and was surprised that he didn't answer since I knew he was expecting me. Around the side of the building, I found another door and knocked again.

This time he answered the door carefully, looking around me for anyone nearby before letting me in.

He was not at all what I pictured him as being. A small, balding man who appeared to be in poor health, he ushered me into an office which was distinguished by its near total lack of furniture, the water stains on the ceiling, and a mattress on the floor near the desk. I sat across from him, not relishing the fact that I had the onerous task of having to go through a list of hundreds of properties in order to analyze their values for an upcoming hearing on real estate taxes that were due on each of them. My eye was drawn to a cockroach scurrying across the floor in one corner of the room.

"I expect you've read the news articles about me?" he began.

"Yes, I have." I answered honestly.

"What opinion have you formed of me?"

"I don't know. We've only just met."

"Good," he said. "Too many individuals make decisions about people they meet based entirely on appearance or what they've heard without ever giving someone the chance to defend themselves."

He went on to explain to me that he believed that the city of Easton and several agencies across eastern Pennsylvania were, for many reasons, harassing him.

One of the primary reasons was that some of his tenants were living in very poor conditions. He explained, however, that he felt he was providing a service for the less fortunate. Rather than being homeless, there were people he was allowing to rent houses for between one hundred fifty dollars and three hundred dollars a month, and hopefully doing some work to fix them up. He rationalized that he could certainly throw the tenants out, renovate the properties, and rent them for six hundred to eight hundred dollars each month But would that be the right thing to do to those tenants who could not afford more than two hundred dollars per month? Would that be the fair thing to do? Would it be better for them to be out living in the streets?

I didn't have an answer for his question. One of the most interesting things I found about Mr. M was that when I met him he was living in his own roach infested tenement.

His bedroom was a mattress on the floor, and although this gentleman had millions of dollars worth of property, he lived just as his tenants did. Not only was he an intriguing character, but he had some interesting stories, one of which concerned his stepmother who he had fallen in love with and married after his father's death.

"You married your step mother?" I asked incredulously.

"Yes," he replied, "but that's not the interesting part of my story."

He had begun buying properties that no one else would touch because there were Department of Welfare liens against them. He said he then sued the government and won by arguing that the Department of Welfare was an agency of the government, not the government itself, and therefore, their liens should have been dissipated in the tax sale.

Mr. M said that he knew the real estate laws far better than the attorneys involved, and that he used that knowledge to regularly and successfully turn the tables on them.

His fortunes had changed a few years earlier, however, when he had had a heart attack, from which he was not expected to live. While Mr. M was incapacitated, his son had sold or transferred to himself dozens of his father's properties, using pre-signed deeds from his father's office. Around the same time, his secretary filed the county's first palimony suit, claiming half of what he owned because she claimed to be living in a marital-like living arrangement. Strangely, Mr. M was not yet fully divorced from his wife, who was also asking for marital property. No one expected him to recover, but he did.

There is another interesting facet of this story. I pulled out my rather lengthy list of the properties, and sat down and told him that I would have to acquaint myself thoroughly with each one.

"The first house," he said, looking at the list, "is 123 Main Street in Easton, Pennsylvania. The tenant's names are Jules and Frannie Kertfelder. I bought the property on March 6th, 1971 for $11,233 at tax sale."

And then, as I listened incredulously, he was able to recite the current tenant's name, their phone number, the current taxes on the property, the amount he paid for the property, the date he bought it, the taxes on the property at the time he purchased the property, and so on.

Furthermore, he was able to do the same thing for all the properties on the list. After the first few, I realized that this was no joke, that he actually knew not only the name of every tenant, but the exact amount of taxes due on every bit of property he owned. He was, to be sure, an eccentric, I suppose, but he was also one of the brightest men I have ever met, and appeared, at least to me, to be quite different from the hard-hearted slum landlord portrayed in the press.

Sadly, he had a heart attack and passed away just outside the courthouse a year later, leaving everything to his sister in California. The litigation went on for more than a decade.

Chapter 10:
Learning from the Past

What Not To Say to a Client

There are times when I'm not the most tactful person in the world. In fact, there are times when even *I* am surprised at what comes out of my mouth. For example, I was once in a real estate workshop in Tampa with over seven hundred agents in the room, when one of my agents was introducing me to a young woman who had flown in the night before from Tennessee.

"Your agent was nice enough to buy me a drink last evening," she said.

"Really?" I replied, "I would have bought you eight."

Everyone within earshot laughed, and although I was kidding, I had a really tough time explaining to my wife what I meant by that comment. There are many days, and this was one of them, when I wonder why my wife puts up with me.

On another occasion several years ago, a client, with whom I had previously worked on selling several investment properties, asked me to look at her primary residence. I had known from prior experience that she held onto "stuff" long past its useful life, but I didn't realize the extent of her pack-rattery until I walked into her home and saw that every inch of the house appeared to be covered with piles of magazines, books, newspapers and boxes of knickknacks. I was surprised the home hadn't already spontaneously combusted from all the old paper. Her decorating, the little that was visible over the mounds, was more than a bit eccentric. It was downright odd. Of course, who am I to judge? I have antique super hero action figures displayed on the wall in my office.

Anyway, the home still retained a bit of character, but it needed significant work, beginning with a good cleaning, fresh paint and some new floor coverings. At the time, I believe I estimated the value at around two hundred thousand dollars. However, Fran explained that she wanted to move to a farm she was purchasing and really wanted five hundred thousand dollars. I told her that it was highly unlikely that she'd receive such a high price, and even if I found someone to pay it, the buyer would probably need to secure a mortgage which meant that the mortgage company would require an appraisal in order to guarantee the lender that there was sufficient value in the home if the buyer defaulted. Also, the appraiser would be likely to look at the same comparable sales that I had, and be likely to come up with a very close number to mine.

Life Lesson: There are more important things in life than money.

It was at that point that Fran let me know she had an offer of twice that amount on the table already. "They're willing to pay me nearly a million dollars," she said.

"If you were offered a million dollars, Fran, take it!" I exclaimed. "But who in the world would pay that much for your home?"

"A developer," she said.

"But you only have an acre," I countered. "What possible

reason would a developer have for wanting this property? Lots are only selling for fifty thousand dollars each and he'd be lucky to get two out of this property."

"The developer bought the land behind me to put up a nursing home," she explained. "But the city told them that they don't have enough land, so they need mine in order to start construction."

"Okay. Well, if they're offering you a million dollars, why would you want to list it for sale for five hundred thousand?"

"Why? Because they'd want to tear down *my* house," she said indignantly. "I couldn't allow that."

"Fran," I said, looking around at the litter of books and magazines, not to mention newspapers. "If someone offered me a million dollars for this home, I wouldn't bother to move the furniture. I'd light the home for them on the way out."

Needless to say, she didn't list with me.

Life's Little Coincidences

Life is filled with coincidences that some call Karma, fate or signs from God. There are stories of coincidence even found in the Bible, like the story of Malachi. Sometimes these coincidences can make the hair on the backs of our necks stand up, as they lead us down long and strange paths.

Anthony Hopkins, for example, was hired to perform in "The Girl from Petrovka," based on a book by George Feifer. Hopkins unsuccessfully searched bookstores across London to locate a copy of the book. As he waited for a train home, he spotted a discarded book on a bench nearby, and, investigating, discovered it was a copy of the book he was seeking, although it was marked up with notes in the margins.[xvii]

During the filming of the movie, a couple years later, Hopkins met the author who identified the book as his own personal copy with his own notes scribbled in the margins. He had lent it to a friend who had lost the book somewhere in London.

A couple represented by Michelle Miller accepted a job relocation to California, selling a home they loved here in Pennsylvania, only to be transferred back a few years later.

For weeks, Michelle showed them house after house, looking for that perfect unique property that they could call home. None of the properties measured up to the one they had sold a few years before, and they were frustrated by the process.

Just when they decided to give up and settle for something that wasn't perfect, their old home came back on the market and they were able to buy it back. Was it coincidence or fate?

The Lingerie Model

Coincidence and what we perceive as fate also leads us to the old adage, "What goes around comes around."

Back in college at Lehigh University, my major was electrical engineering, with marketing as my minor. In our marketing class, we were broken into teams, each of which had to come up with a project that would include a full advertising program or marketing campaign, including copies of ads, on the basis of which we would be graded.

Some teams were assigned an innocuous product like soap, but ours was, of all things, women's lingerie. After much discussion we settled on magazine style ads, billboard style ads and a commercial, but we could not agree on whether we should simply go out and buy lingerie, and take photographs of the products in order to create these billboard style ads and magazine style ads or use a model.

Initially, we agreed simply to purchase several articles of lingerie and create mock-up ads, a tactic which presented a challenge because our entire group was male. But we managed and created a series of ads based on photographs of bra and panties on a dark background. Unfortunately, the ads had no real appeal, and our team agreed that this marketing campaign was not going result in A's all around. So, we punted back to plan B, and opted to hire a model.

After locating one, we scheduled a day for her to meet with us at my fraternity, Alpha Lambda Omega.   The model posed for us in one of the common rooms on the second floor, wearing her own lingerie, something she had insisted on, which turned out to be even more revealing than what we would have chosen.

The guys on our team carefully decorated everything around her, and prepared to do the photos and accompanying video by setting up cameras and a beta-max video camera on tripods around the room. And since we were running out of time to get our project turned in, we were anxious to get this done in a single afternoon.

When the fire alarm went off, we all froze. In the nearly four years that I was at Alpha Lambda Omega I had never, ever heard a fire alarm or engaged in a fire drill. No one moved. And then, assuming that it was a fire drill, we continued what we were doing. Ten minutes later, we were discovered by a fire marshal who was clearly astonished to find four young men engaged in filming a scantily clothed woman.

He, of course, called campus security who promptly picked us up, since having a half naked female in our fraternity house was a definite no-no.

It is interesting how much college life has changed over the past two decades. For example, had one of our students at Lehigh run naked through a quad, they would surely have been expelled. Recently, another university was reported to have hired lawyers to defend several college students who streaked through town, and were arrested for indecent exposure. The university wanted to protect the student's "right to free speech." My, how the world has changed, but once again I digress.

We had a very difficult time explaining that we were actually doing a required class project. Eventually, we had to get our professor on the phone to come down and explain. He had a good laugh at our expense, and ultimately rewarded us with a high grade on our project.

Here's the coincidental part. Several years later I was working in the field of computer engineering at a software firm. One morning, our lingerie model walked into the office and was introduced to everyone as a new programmer for the company. At this point I was still young and fairly stupid when it comes to the way people relate to each other in life. Software companies tend to attract fairly geeky men, and many of them found the young lady quite attractive. After a few days of working with her, I made the mistake of bringing copies of the photographs in to work to show some of the other guys.

What I didn't realize at that point was that one of the primary reasons she was working for the firm was she had become engaged to my boss. This was one of the few jobs in my life from which I was outright fired.

There were actually two life lessons I learned from this experience. First, you never know when something you do in your life will come back to haunt you. I'm sorry to admit that this young woman took modeling jobs to help pay her own way through school and was embarrassed by some of her younger indiscretions. Keep that in mind, dear readers, when you text your photo to

> *Life Lesson:*
> *There is **never** a good reason to show off at the expense of someone else. Live by the Golden Rule.*

your latest boyfriend or girlfriend. With the phenomenal growth of the Internet, nearly any piece of data on anyone can be located.

Many young women today publish all sorts of photos of themselves, often for the benefit of a boyfriend, believing there's nothing wrong with what they "put out there". The truth, however, is that, at some point, many of these young women, looking to make a place for themselves in the corporate world, will find that bosses and co-workers, not to mention a future husband or children will often find these pictures online with unfortunate results all around.

The second lesson I learned from this experience was a personal one. In trying to ingratiate myself to some co-workers or make myself look "cool," I hurt someone else. There is never a reason to show off at the expense of someone else. None of us is without sin. I've made too many mistakes to count, and I am never pleased when they come back to haunt me. The golden rule of life is, "Do unto others as you'd want others to do to you."

Misleading Real Estate Terms

Last year, I showed a home that was only one hundred to one hundred fifty feet from a gigantic electrical power tower to a potential buyer who was enraged that I would even consider the possibility that it would be an acceptable property. After all, haven't I read all the articles about how these big towers may cause cancer, sterility, and possibly attract travelers from other dimensions? In the end, he managed to work himself into such a frenzy that he actually attacked my profession in general. I should, he said, have tried to dissuade buyers from viewing the property, not encourage them.

I understood his point, but I also realized that my job was to sell the property and I couldn't do that if I couldn't get buyers to look at it. My response, of course, was to remind him that I was representing the owner and that it was my job to present the property in the best light, admitting, at the time, that it was sometimes necessary to walk a fine line. However, there had been – and I stressed this – no misrepresentation.

Interestingly, this particular buyer ultimately decided that the positives of the home outweighed the negative and made an offer. I refrained from pointing out that if the property had been presented in a negative light, he would never have seen it.

In real estate advertising, as in any other, misleading statements abound. Some realtors try to put positive spins on home features that are somewhat less than positive. Please don't misunderstand me. A conveniently located, cozy and charming home with easy highway access that needs a little TLC might be a great starter home for a family with a little bit of paint. Sadly, too many realtors use these words in other ways.

In fact, a leading real estate trainer actually promotes using "the term cozy instead of small" and "charming instead of old" as a method of attracting buyers. This practice is called 'puffing.' The following is a list of some of the best examples of inappropriately used words.

- **Cozy** – One of my favorite terms. It means the home is too small for human habitation. Remember the 19th Century when a family of six could live in a single room home? This is the home for them.

- **Intimate** – The only home smaller than 'cozy.' These homes are perfect if you're roughly the size of a garden gnome.

- **Charming** – If you're used to living without indoor plumbing, this home is perfect for you. It comes complete with old woodwork, wide molding, and kitchen cabinets that date before the Great Depression. The cobwebs are an added bonus.

- **Conveniently Located** – It is located at a busy intersection, where the traffic noise is so heavy, you'll have to sleep with ear plugs.

- **Easy Highway Access** – This is actually worse than "Conveniently Located". Here you'll have to sleep with pillows duct taped to your head.

- **Country Living** – We hope you like spending a lot of time driving because this home is located so far from civilization that you may have to raise your own animals in order to survive.

- **City Living-** Lock the doors with all three deadbolts because it's not safe to go outside.

- **Needs Some TLC** – Beware. You might fall through the floor.

- **Water View** – If you stand on a ladder in the corner bedroom of the second floor and lean out the window, you might be able to see it.

- **Water Front** - Located in a flood zone.

- **Not a Drive-By** – Because the exterior is so hideous, you're likely to drive by without stopping. You might even look over your shoulder to see if condemned signs have been placed in the yard yet.

- **Must See The Inside** – This is a variation of "Not a Drive-By." The outside looks like it's been decorated for

Halloween, but it's currently March. The Addams Family actually turned this home down.

- **Handyman Special** – So special that not even the walls are solid. The home is probably ready to collapse.

- **Unique** – This home is so unique that it will only appeal to a small percentage of the population. In fact, the number of buyers who would appreciate the architecture is so small that we're still hoping some weird person from southern California takes a job relocation and moves to the area.

- **Easy to Show** – The prior owners vacated the home as soon as they heard the gunfire down the street. The doors don't shut properly, so pretty much anyone can go in anytime they'd like.

- **Only One Owner** – And he didn't make an update since the day he built the home forty-seven years ago.

- **Freshly Painted** – With a single coat of cheap paint.

- **Cul-de-sac Living** – A fancy way to say you'll be living at a 'dead-end.'

- **Friendly Neighborhood** – In fact, several busy bodies will watch your every move and the creepy guy across the street has a telescope trained on this home at all times.

Chapter 11:
Society, Politics and Economics

Lately, I've been wondering, whatever happened to morality? At a dinner recently, one of the men made a suggestive comment about one of the women at the table, clearly embarrassing her, upon which some of the other women started teasing her for being a prude. Didn't we used to scold the man for making such comments? Why is it an issue for a woman to have some modicum of decorum?

One of the more interesting conversations I have had recently was with a young woman who was pregnant with her boyfriend's child, prompting yet another of my famous faux pas.

"Oh, congratulations," I said. "Are you planning to get married?"

I knew my question was a mistake before it completely left my mouth, but I wasn't prepared for the answer.

"Of course not," she replied. "Having a child is one thing, but I'm not ready for the commitment of a marriage."

Wow, when did society flip the family model that far?

In another situation, a heated discussion in our office lobby resulted when one of our employees explained that one of her clients periodically slept with her ex-husband, even though she was now married to someone else. This was, she claimed, what was referred to as a "booty call."   In the face of fairly vigorous protests from one of the other office agents, she presented the argument that past partners have every right to renew relationships no matter what their present marital status. Again, I can't understand how anyone at all can think this way, much less try to defend such a position. Perhaps it's a result of too much reality television, or perhaps it's the Britney Spears Song, *Living in Sin is the New In*!

We learn what is normal from those around us and from those inputs we allow into our homes and mind. The television and internet teach us what others are doing and what society's expectations include. Among other things, this has lead to an increased sexualization of society. For example, we are bombarded on a daily basis with images of scantily clad women.

Sadly, as a society, we're becoming less and less modest. Let's be honest, we all know that sex sells. What used to be stretching the limits of propriety in beer commercials has been transferred to virtually every magazine cover on the racks, and advertising for virtually every industry. Nearly nude women appear in ads for soaps, clothing, perfume, deodorant, computer software, web hosting, pizza, tacos, and even milk. In fact, in a European commercial for eye doctors, a woman actually performs oral sex on a car's stick shift. Apparently, she missed the man because she lacked the proper prescription glasses.

Of course, the Internet opens us up to taking this a step further until what was once considered immoral may well come to seem to be nothing out of the ordinary. One study shows that Internet porn earns more per year than Microsoft, Google, eBay and Amazon combined. That's incredible.

Please don't misunderstand me. I love the female figure. I believe it's hardwired into our brains, but do we really need to be constantly titillated?

It's also interesting what has become important to us. For example, a young couple, James O'Keefe and Hannah Giles, posing as a pimp and a prostitute, recently ran a series of "sting" operations on a group called Acorn, the Association of Community Organizers for Reform Now, whose various purposes include fair housing and raising the minimum wage. According to news reports, in California, New York, Maryland and even Washington D.C., workers at this organization attempted to advise the young couple on such things as how to set up a house of prostitution for underage girls brought in from South America as well as how to claim the ill-gotten profits on their taxes and purchase real estate with the proceeds.[xviii] This is the same group accused of voter fraud across the county, and yet was one of the groups that was supposed to split over eight billion dollars from the 2009 stimulus package in addition to the huge funding it already drew from government agencies.

O'Keefe and Giles have hours of video online showing *many* Acorn workers at a number of locations trying to help set up this illegal business. The video didn't show up on prime time news shows because the country was far too busy talking about an outburst by Kanye West at the MTV music awards and about new hybrid cars helping to reduce global warming. Perhaps it's time to start paying attention to the issues that are dragging us down.

Society is changing at breakneck speed. In glorifying reality television, we allow ourselves to be entertained by the pain of others. We watch as young starlets attempt to improve their Google rankings by "accidentally" flashing the paparazzi, while we ignore the real challenges our country is facing. We listen to sound bites on the news, accept them as gospel and then try to defend them to others without really understanding what's happening in the world.

Is It Getting Darker?

A year ago in mid February, I received a well written email announcing that we're all doomed because the world was going to be plunged into darkness. The writer claimed to have been carefully and accurately tracking how much daylight we were experiencing each day and had discovered that, since autumn, daylight had been reduced by about two minutes per day. At that current rate, he claimed, the earth would be in total darkness by late summer. Without the ability to photosynthesize, all plant life would die, followed by all other life on earth.

> *Life Lesson:*
> *Follow the flow of the money. It will often lead you to the truth.*

Of course, it was absolutely true that there were two minutes less of daylight every single day for the prior few months, but as most people know, because the earth moves through cycles, during autumn and winter, daylight is reduced each day. During spring and summer, we experience more daylight because the cycle shifts. This hysteria we create for ourselves by taking one piece of evidence and building a catastrophic theory around it is what I call "fuzzy logic."

Virtually every government agency across the globe agrees that global warming is a reality because the average temperature is $7/10^{th}$ of one degree warmer than it was one hundred years ago and if we don't act quickly, we'll all die a terrible and hideous death with lots of screaming, begging and crying. Basically, they say, the earth is getting warmer because humans and animals are breathing out carbon dioxide, thereby increasing our carbon footprint on the earth. This situation is apparently compounded by the fact that many of us are driving great big SUV's which also hurt the environment by sending a variant, carbon monoxide, into the atmosphere.

Much of the theory of global warming is not based on observation, but rather on computer modeling which many scientists agree is severely flawed, particularly since the world continues to get cooler and has done so for the past ten years. A climate computer model sounds good because it sounds high tech, right? And it must be true, because we've all seen the video of the polar bear stuck on a chunk of ice, floating out to sea. Actually, I'm surprised more people don't point out that polar bears can swim for very long distances so the polar bear on the ice was not in danger.

The computer model, which is based on information available today, predicts that the earth's temperature will rise, accelerate, the polar caps will melt and that we're all doomed unless we do something right now. The interesting problem with this computer model is that we can prove it doesn't work. We already *have* historical data to test and it doesn't work. If we plug in all the numbers from twenty years ago and try to predict today's temperatures, or any climate changes, it doesn't actually predict what we're experiencing right now. If we plug in CO^2 levels from thirty years ago, it also doesn't predict the temperature or global climate. So if the model won't predict current conditions from information we already know, how can we possibly expect it to be accurate about the future?

The truth is that, although thousands of scientists don't believe in global warming, they are silent because those who have written articles about its non-existence are ridiculed and ignored by the media. After all, a crisis brings lots of money to special interest groups and businesses, and crises bring power to those in the government, power that allows government agencies to oversee industry and take over industries on a national level, "for the good of the world". The "threat" of global warming brings a lot of money and resources to scientists who research it, as well as being a boon to newspapers and televisions, attracting audiences that number in the millions.

Here's a thought that most people seem to forget: we can prove that at least three ice ages have occurred in the past. One of these may have been the reason for the extinction of dinosaurs. If we *know three* ice ages took place, and that the warming periods that followed couldn't have been caused by our SUV's or aerosol cans and the like because none of that existed back then, then perhaps the earth simply goes through periods of heating and cooling? That would make more sense. Perhaps our warming trends in the late 1980s and early 1990s had to do with significant and measurable solar activity, which is what actually heats our atmosphere? More importantly, if the earth really does go through periods of heating and cooling, just like seasons, then what *is* the correct temperature of the earth? Is it the temperature we're feeling today? Is it the temperatures we experienced one hundred years ago? Is it the temperature from one thousand years ago?

I have two more thoughts on global warming. Have you noticed that each day the weather men report what the record temperatures for that day were in history, as in, "The record temperature for this day in history was set in 1961?" Have you noticed that the record temperature always seems to have happened sometime in the past?

Secondly, the average temperatures have cooled down for the last eleven years. Look it up. It is cooler on average today than it was a decade ago and yet we're still crazy about global warming. What about all that melting ice? There are some areas of ice that are melting seasonally. There are also areas that are freezing and where ice is continually growing. According to a January 2009 report from the Science and Public Policy Institute, "The rate of sea-ice formation in October 2008 was the most rapid ever observed."[xix]

I might mention one other interesting report on average temperature readings that was done by Glenn Beck of Fox News. While researching the thermometers that are used to accurately measure temperature change, the team found that some thermometers were directly over blacktop, which raises the heat register, as well as being blown on by heating ducts and located on the top of buildings, always the hottest spots. A few months later, Beck reported on hundreds of emails between recognized climate change scientists that were stolen from a computer server at a British University.

The long list of emails exchanged between climate researchers included one from "Phil Jones, a longtime climate researcher at the East Anglia Climate Research Unit, [who said] he had used a 'trick' employed by another scientist, Michael Mann [of Penn State], to 'hide the decline' in temperatures."[xx]

I'll leave you with one other thought regarding the supposed threat of global warming. Perhaps you'll remember that in the late 1970s, not only were we about to suffer an imminent nuclear attack that was about to destroy the world, but we were also being doomed by acid rain and the new ice age which was rapidly approaching. And do you remember the hysteria that greeted the first Earth Day in 1970 when it was announced that there was proof that a new ice age was upon us? Run a search of old articles in *Newsweek*, *Time* and *The New York Times*. There are plenty of great articles.

In fact, if you go back even further, you'll find that in 1924, *The*

> *Life Lesson:*
> *What we believe is far more real to us than reality.*

New York Times ran articles warning of scientific evidence of "global cooling" and a new ice age.[xxi] There were claims that we had absolute proof that we would all freeze to death. In the 1930s, the same newspaper warned us of warming trends caused by mankind and that we were now destroying the earth and causing global warming. On April 28th, 1975, *Newsweek* dispelled the idea of global warming by proving that the temperature of the earth had cooled from 1940 to 1975 and announced the advent of the next ice age.

Even the global warming proponents are realizing that they may have a problem and are changing the language to "global climate change" which will now feature hurricanes, tornados and earth quakes. Of course, we've always experienced those, but now we can blame it on people.

Please don't mistake my criticism of the pseudo-science of global warming as an attack on environmental responsibility. I have four children, and would love to leave them a clean and pure earth with no medical waste floating in the ocean off the coast of New Jersey, no cancer causing agents being pumped up from our wells, and fat free cupcakes that actually have some taste. But we need to have open and honest discussions about the challenges facing the world, not hysteria.

The Auto Manufacturers

Life's lessons can come from anywhere. We never stop learning. Many of my greatest "aha's" were lessons I learned on the street or in business. Some lessons, however, we learn in the classrooms of educational institutions, from both the instructors and from watching our peers. Recently I listened to a professor lecture about business communication and employee motivation.

The professor loaded a Power Point slide which featured a single frame editorial cartoon showing an assembly line in a car manufacturing plant on a giant screen behind her. On one side of the cartoon was an executive, wearing a hat that said "CEO" and a t-shirt with the saying "Golden Parachute" on it, who was pointing at a line worker putting a tire onto a car. The caption read something like, "The reason our company is going under is that people like you are demanding middle income wages and health benefits."

When the professor asked for a reaction, one of the students explained that she didn't feel that $70 an hour in salary and benefits for a line worker in the automotive industry was a "middle income wage".

The professor appeared to be taken aback by the comment. "You do realize that the CEOs of these companies are making millions and millions in salary, bonuses and stock options," she said and went on to point out that, should the line worker incorrectly mount the tire, someone might be killed in an accident. "In fact," she continued, "it can be argued that the line worker's position may be more important than that of the CEO."

> *Life Lesson:*
> *We have a tendency to label each other, rather than see the whole picture.*

"That may be true," the student countered, "and perhaps the CEO's salary is too high as well. However, there are a whole lot more employees earning $70 an hour than there are CEO's earning millions of dollars. And the company pays far more in wages and benefits to workers than to management."

The student continued by explaining that she was completing an MBA at this prestigious university and was still earning less than $15 an hour in middle management at a moderate sized company.

Some of these linemen, few of them as well educated as she, were making much more than she was, while living in a far less expensive area.

I always have difficulty analyzing this situation because I'm of the opinion that companies should be allowed to offer whatever wage they wish to prospective employees. Likewise, every employee should be allowed to ask whatever he or she wants to be paid for the job. That creates a negotiation situation which should result in workers being paid based on supply and demand.

Too many union people believe that if there isn't a minimum wage in every company, if there isn't a requirement for how much the company must pay through a union contract, management would only be paying one dollar an hour to every employee on the floor.

The reality is that corporations compete for good workers and then keep them based on their merit or performance.

One of the main reasons that employees move from area to area is to better their incomes, and improve their lives, and in some cases, from country to country to find better work. Alternately, companies move, as well, in search of lower costs and highly motivated workers.

Foreign Competition

We always have to look at what we're doing in our lives as having consequences beyond our physical boundaries. Whether we're a small town that has a manufacturing plant down the street, or a part of a large multinational corporation, we have to understand that there are rules being changed every day across the globe and we have to be able and willing to deal with them.

Several years ago, I read an interview with the CEO of a company which manufactured appliances who said that he was moving some of his operations to Mexico in order to put his company in a better competitive position. At one point in time, the company was doing very well and had been one of the country's top appliance manufacturers. He paid his workers a great salary for the work they did and everyone was happy and danced in the street and butterflies crossed prairies and so forth. When those appliances began to be made in China and Mexico, they were, of course, brought into the United States at a much lower price since the workers in these countries are paid much lower wages, sometimes as little as seventeen cents an hour. Big box stores picked up these appliances as lower priced alternatives to the American made appliances.

In order to compete, the CEO of the American company started a "Buy American" campaign. However, despite their best efforts, the number of appliances this company sold continued to dwindle until the company's ranking dropped significantly. Income was down and the company was rapidly losing market share because consumers were simply purchasing the lower priced alternatives. Why spend twice as much on a dishwasher when both units wash your dirty dishes?

The CEO held a meeting and told everyone that he had been left with only two tough choices. The company could no longer compete against appliance manufacturers in China and Mexico, because they couldn't entice consumers to buy the American made products at a higher price. Consumers were all shopping at Walmart and Best Buy, purchasing the lower cost alternatives, which they believed to be the best value. This was, he reminded them, the same way the textiles business virtually vanished from America in the 50s.

Since the company could not manufacture them in the United States and sell them at a price point that would be competitive with other manufacturers, the choices were either to keep going the way they were until the company eventually was forced to declare bankruptcy, in which case, the current employees would lose their jobs and the U.S. factories would close. Or they could compete with the other appliance manufacturers by building the products in China and Mexico themselves, in which case, although most of the current employees would lose their jobs, some would be able to remain in shipping, distribution, management, service and so on.

Either way, the workers will lose. The question was whether or not the company would survive, still employing some white collar workers and doing what was best for the stock holders.

Incidentally, I'm not pretending to have the answers to this dilemma. I don't know exactly what the right move might be in a situation like this. I have a fairly strong background in finance and economics, but it doesn't mean that I have all the solutions.

What I *do* understand, however, is that we can more often succeed if we try to understand both sides of an issue rather than taking a side that benefits us most and trying to argue it against all reason.

CEO Salaries, Bonuses and Stock Options, Oh My!

Enron executives artificially inflated their corporate earnings in order to increase their stock options and bonuses and tried to abscond with people's money. There are a number of cases of executives like these that have effectively cooked the books on a large scale for their personal benefit. Ultimately, they are caught, of course, and these types of executives aren't the ones I want to focus on in my attempt to play the devil's advocate, although I realize some of these salaries and bonuses are obscene.

However, there's another way to look at this situation. Football players earn millions of dollars based on how well they play and how much money they can bring to the stadium, the team and the owners through attracting patrons. The owners of the football team want to win, and want to make a profit, or a return on the money they've invested in buying and improving the team. Football players earn these salaries because they are the only ones talented enough to play the game we want to see.

A corporation exists partly to produce a return for the stockholders, who are the people who invest in the corporation. Incidentally, anyone who has money in a retirement plan, a pension fund or in a life insurance policy is likely to be invested in these companies through the purchase of stock. Our saving's, or our retirement portfolio's growth is based on how well these companies perform. So when you talk about the rich who own corporations, remember that you may be one of those owners. Companies, like baseball teams, are trying to produce something of value and stay in business at the same time. That value may be a service or it may be a product.

In any case, corporations, be they General Motors, General Electric or Walmart, want to hire the best, most talented individuals possible to manage a multibillion dollar company. Hopefully, the individuals in charge will make their companies so profitable that their stock will gain value, thus enabling the holders of this stock to profit accordingly.

Certainly, no one can argue the fact that a CEO who improves the bottom line of a company by five hundred million dollars is not worth the twenty-five million he is being paid.

There's another way to consider this subject. If you really need a particular key person in order to propel the company forward and you know that that key person who is going to benefit the company in the long term to the tune of several billion dollars, is being offered twenty-four million dollars from a competitor, is it then worth your while to offer him twenty-five million to guarantee that he will stay with you?

No one argues that the Yankees should not pay Alex Rodriguez over thirty million dollars, or Shaq twenty million for his basketball skills or for that matter, Johnny Depp thirty-five million per film. The public thinks these individuals are worth their huge paychecks, but highly skilled and educated executives are viewed differently.

I can't give you an answer to that question, but I don't believe that in a free society, we have the right to set limits on what people can and should earn based on the opinions of politicians in Washington or anyone who wants to stick it to the rich. Just because you or I may think that these executives earn too much doesn't mean that they actually do.

If we're limiting people's income, shouldn't we then limit the amount of money that's given out on the Powerball or any other lottery?

"Well, Loren, now you're getting crazy," you may say. "That's different. The higher the Powerball, the more people play the game, which benefits all sorts of great causes," to which I'll reply, "So if you get $100 million dollars on Powerball, that's completely different. Really? You didn't do anything to win the lottery, except buy a one dollar ticket from the local mini-mart or gas station. And really, if you won $10 million instead of $100 million, what really is the difference in lifestyle to you?

Right now, you're earning $45,000 per year. So a ten million dollar bump in your income this year would immediately improve your financial condition, wouldn't it? Shouldn't the other ninety million go back to the government to be distributed to whoever the government feels is deserving of your money this week?

Again, I don't have an answer to this question. It's an imponderable. I'm also one of those crazy people who believe that a lot of the money the government confiscates and gives to federal programs is designed to buy voters and benefit certain segments of society.

Taking Away the Punchbowl

A friend of mine in Lehigh University's finance department, Geraldo Vasconcellos, has told me on more than one occasion that it's difficult to be the voice of reason in a world of emotion. He likens it to a good party that's really going strong, but getting out of hand, and someone has to be the adult and take away the punch bowl. I love that analogy, so I'd like to borrow it here.

Our country is spending far more than it "earns" in taxes. In order to create more and more government programs, buy more votes, and seize more control over our lives, our businesses and our property, they have had to borrow trillions of dollars. Spending one trillion dollars, by the way, is *more* than spending one million dollars a day, every single day, from the birth of Jesus until today.

Something that we too often forget is that the government does not have any money of their own. Again, *the government doesn't have any money.* The U.S. Government, State Governments, local governments and agencies all have to find a way to secure the money they spend. There are several ways this happens. The first is for government agencies to confiscate money from us in taxes and fees. The second is to borrow money from us, by selling bonds, or get it from China, Japan, Dubai, and the rest of the world, and pay interest or we can always print money, which is the equivalent of creating it out of thin air.

Starting with the last method of obtaining money, since we are living in a global economy, if the Government prints lots of money, it devalues the dollar which means that inflation drives the overall value of our currency down. That means that the dollar that once purchased a bottle of Diet Coke now only purchases half that and that also means that every product at Walmart that's made in China now costs more in terms of U.S. dollars.

Actually, borrowing money is what is absolutely killing us as a nation. Remember that the country is made up of all of us, so we should all be concerned when we find ourselves in a position of owing trillions of dollars to foreign countries to whom we have sold U.S. bonds which must, in the future, be repaid with interest. Let me explain it a different way. If we didn't "earn" enough money to fund all the U.S. government's programs this year and had to borrow the money to balance the budget, then next year, we would not only face an expanded budget, which we can't afford, but debts to foreign countries on top of it. So we print more bonds, sell them and create even more debt, which is just like maxing out a credit card and taking out two more credit cards to pay off the last one.

At some point this madness has to end if we don't want the country to go bankrupt. According to Glenn Beck's research team from Fox News, our payment on that debt amounts to over $312 billion per year.[xxii] That number may not mean anything to you, but imagine the biggest company you can. Is it Walmart? Their *total* profit last year was only $40 billion. Even if the government confiscated all their earnings, they would barely pay a fraction of the *interest* on the debt we have created. We're not talking about paying the debt. We're talking about paying the *interest* on the outstanding debt.

All that remains, therefore is taxation which is a problem because the government is already taking a substantial percentage of the income of Americans through taxation. Consider this: your company pays huge taxes to the federal government. Your company then pays you and you pay taxes. You buy products that have taxes built in because the government is taking 35-40% of every dollar every company makes, so they have to raise prices to incorporate those taxes.

And there are so many of them. You stop for gas on the way home, and there's hidden tax on every gallon you pump. You buy products at the store and pay sales tax. You pay school and property taxes for the privilege of living on your own land. If you buy liquor or cigarettes, the taxes are incredible. Add each of those up and divide them by your gross income and figure out how much of your money is being taken by the government. Now consider what you might have been able to do with that same money. At the same time, you might think about all the waste and corruption and realize that you're helping to fund it. We're on a path that I believe is unsustainable.

Government agencies everywhere are nearly bankrupt from overspending. California is simply one example of what happens when we buy into the argument that more and more government is the answer to everything. After all, politicians enjoy being given the power to dole out funds.

Gambling is suddenly okay virtually everywhere, because in many parts of the country, the government gets more than half the money. I'm not getting on a soap box about gambling because I have gambled in Las Vegas and Atlantic City at a time when it was heavily regulated. But now, the government wants its share of the pot. Forget everyone it hurts, because it's revenue to the government. Smoking and drinking give them a lot of cash, too, so their taxing our vices. How long until they determine that illegal drugs and prostitution will create a windfall and determine they're acceptable everywhere as well?

Many Americans seem to want to have a nanny state, in which they are taken care of by the government. This scares me more than anything else. We have changed from a pioneering people to a people who look to Washington for all the answers instead of looking to ourselves. Whatever happened to self-sufficiency? Why does everyone seem to need a handout? Why are we willing to relinquish the freedoms that our forefathers fought *so* hard for in return for a few scraps from the government?

So many of my clients, my friends and my relatives demand that the politicians in Washington do something to fix our economy, our health care, our student loans, our mortgage interest rates and everything else. While, as I said earlier, we should recognize that we live in a global economy, we also have to realize that the government is nothing more than a big business, run primarily by attorneys and politicians, giving them the power to tax and the power to regulate everyone else. Our government was intentionally designed *by the people, for the people*, not by the state to rule everybody under them.

Every week, in the paper and online, we read stories about corruption, payoffs and greed. Politicians giving away something to their friends in exchange for helping them get elected. Why would anyone trust people like this to run our lives? Are we really willing to trade our freedoms for the government providing jobs, healthcare and shelter?

This is called socialism, a system that has failed time and time again. Part of the reason it fails is that it eliminates any benefits from hard work, and part of the reason is that it gives people at the top of the pyramid of government the belief that they are all-powerful. Look at the old Soviet Union, China, and even Cuba. Do the people truly benefit from this kind of rule?

Today's latest crisis appears to be healthcare, although everyone is skewing the numbers to benefit themselves. "It's a right," people cry. Not too many years ago, health insurance was only available for catastrophic illness like cancer, so the expense was not high. People would go to doctors and pay a small fee for service. Then patients began to initiate lawsuits which forced doctors to take out such costly insurance that the patient's cost for doctor's visits grew and grew. And then, as if this were not enough, in comes the government. Suddenly everything had to be done according to government regulation, paperwork must be filed, coding must be done. All this had led to a dramatic increase in staffing, storage and space for medical practitioners. Once again, the cost went up.

So instead of trying to fix the system, we ask for universal health insurance. Ultimately, however, the money the government spends on health care comes from us, so once again they will have to raise taxes and borrow money. Instead of paying insurance companies directly, we pay our bureaucracy, even though we know how well it does with every program it touches.

Social Security is nearly bankrupt. I don't know anyone if anyone still believes that Social Security will be around in its current form in twenty years. Medicare is also nearly bankrupt and even the U.S. Postal Service is hemorrhaging money and trying to cut back on service, so why not add another huge program when they can't even fix the ones they've been working on for decades?

In 2009, I thought it was entertaining to see politicians explain why they were better prepared to run a healthcare program than medical professionals. The entertaining part was that at the same time they spoke about health care, they introduced the "Cash for Clunkers" program, which was supposed to cost one billion dollars, last a few months and help save both the environment and the auto industry.

What happened was that they had to freeze the "Cash for Clunkers" program because too many people were taking advantage of the free money. That would never happen with healthcare, would it? Then they restarted it, but had to raise the government subsidy to three billion, three times the original estimate, only weeks before the program, which was shorted by a month, came to an end. After that, car dealers complained that the government misprocessed paperwork, making it very difficult to get the reimbursement money they were promised and in general creating havoc. It is not reassuring to see that they could not even handle a simple program like this efficiently.

Going back to my original point, the only way to make everything, including health care, "free" in this country is to take away everyone's income and assets and redistribute them in a way that seems fair to one segment of society. In addition, it would create a system which, because of the impossibility of providing everything for everyone would ultimately lead to rationing.

Secondarily, if there's no system of incentives that benefit an individual for their hard work, many will determine that there's no real reason to work harder. This is the problem with our current welfare system, one that allows people to sit home and earn nearly as much as they did when they were working. Consequently, it stands to reason, that there being no reason for these people to work hard, many will not work at all, with the result that productivity will be reduced, thus reducing the size of the pie which we must all share, and leading ultimately to rationing.

As I've said earlier in this book, I believe in the human spirit. I believe in the ability of the individual to rise up and create a better world for himself and for those around him.

Chapter 12:
The Lighter Side of Real Estate

We Forgot Grandma

We have all heard the stories of large families forgetting one of their children at an amusement park, or of a school bus pulling out from a class trip less one student. Film maker John Hughes made a lot of money from his hugely successful *Home Alone* movie franchise depicting a child accidentally left behind when the child's family took a Christmas vacation.

A few years ago, our team experienced a similar situation first hand. Mike and Michelle Miller, who I introduced earlier in this book, purchased a home in Salisbury, Pennsylvania. The home needed some work and had a few challenges, but it was spacious and fit the Miller's lifestyle at the time. You see, Mike and Michelle have eight children. Although most of them are now grown, I can't imagine what school shopping must have been like, but I digress.

Following settlement, Mike, Michelle and assorted family and friends pulled trucks up to their new house, opened the front door, and gave a rowdy family cheer. Over the following hour, they unloaded furniture and boxes for the main living areas on the first floor.

When they reached the second floor, and opened the bedroom doors, they discovered that the prior owner's grandmother was still in bed, and for that matter, was still in the home. The former owners planned to move her last and hadn't wanted to disturb her until the final part of the move. Sadly, they appeared to have forgotten her during their final packing.

It took nearly six hours for the prior owner to come back and retrieve grandma and her belongings.

Stuffed Animals

On another occasion, Mike and Michelle were showing properties to clients who were professional ball room dance instructors, and very successful at their trade. The final showing of the afternoon was a massive Bucks County estate owned by a big game hunter. The main level of the multimillion dollar home was overflowing with huge animals from around the world, including tiger cubs and some recent acquisitions from an African expedition.

Although the owner's wife had instructed Mike, Michelle and the buyers not to touch anything, Mike had become entranced with how alive the animals looked and was having difficulty not touching them. Entering the great room, he discovered that some of the animal's noses appeared to be wet, and, unable to stop himself, reached to check. The owner slapped Mike's hand, causing some embarrassment and a sincere apology.

The group mounted the stairs to the second floor and proceeded into the large master bedroom suite. Just inside the door, Mike noticed the family dog was looking up at him. On the bed lay a cat, stretched out in the afternoon sunlight streaming through the windows. Mike moved to pet the dog, and Michelle the cat, only to discover they were both stuffed as well.

The Midnight Settlement

Early in my career, our company represented an unscrupulous buyer who found a loophole in his purchase agreement that allowed him to cancel the sale. Just before settlement, and just after the home seller had moved all their belongings, Fred dropped this bombshell on the owner. He attempted to renegotiate the sale to a drastically reduced price by the threat of walking away from the purchase.

The seller, who was moving out of state, had to decide whether it was worth paying two mortgages for several months until he found another buyer, or be held hostage to the current buyer. Both sides lawyered up, and argued about the validity of the buyer's loophole.

Ultimately, the seller agreed to a lower price and the buyer agreed to settle, but both wanted their attorney to handle settlement and couldn't agree on a time for consummation of the transaction. Finally, with all parties yelling at each other on a conference call, someone suggested that if we couldn't come up with a suitable time when everyone was free, we could always settle at midnight. The seller's attorney, clearly agitated, responded with 'fine.'

I called my father, who was vacationing in Canada at the time, to let him know the latest crazy thing that was happening, and he one-upped me. He and the rest of my family had narrowly escaped from a charging bull by driving his car very fast down a long, winding road backward. Hmm, perhaps unusual circumstances *do* run in families.

Ray the Roofer

Ray was one of the best of old-time craftsmen, from his knowledge of every type of roof material and installation method to his careful application of each roof. During the nearly two decades he worked with our firm before his passing, he installed hundreds of roofs of every type.

On one occasion, however, we were pressed to have repairs done for a re-inspection in order to settle a property. The FHA appraiser had required a new flat roof be placed on a west Allentown row home prior to settlement, and we could not extend settlement because the buyer's were moving out of an apartment and had nowhere to go.

Ray went out early in the morning with the intention of finishing the entire roof by late afternoon, giving us sufficient time to complete settlement. Just after 3 pm, I met the inspector at the home and met Ray as he was coming down the ladder. The job was done quickly, and was a beautiful job. Unfortunately, it was the wrong house. He was one door too far south.

Pumpkins and Flags

In the real estate industry and many other sales professions, the term 'farming' refers to selecting a neighborhood or a group of people and contacting them regularly until that group begins to consider the salesperson as 'their' salesperson. Farming can be an extraordinarily effective method of building business for a realtor, but it generally only works if the realtor diligently maintains contact for a minimum of twelve to eighteen months. Few realtors are willing to invest the time and energy into the project.

One of America's top sales trainers, Tom Hopkins, has told a story across the country of how he purchased a truckload of pumpkins, gathered some neighborhood children, and delivered them to each home in his 'farm' just before Halloween. Neighborhood kids were excited as he came down the street with his load of pumpkins, their parents came outside, and he was able to introduce himself personally.

This technique set him apart from every other realtor in town who simply mailed information or ran advertisements. Realtors across the country have tried reproducing his success for the past several decades.

At a real estate workshop in the early 1990's, the speaker told a story of how the primary competitor to his firm ordered thousands of pumpkins that they intended to deliver in the middle of the night. The pumpkins were to be delivered without any card suggesting who left them, beginning a campaign of 'who left the pumpkins' which would ultimately lead to a big announcement later in the week. The speaker admitted that he had received a tip about the campaign and felt it would hurt his business, so he quietly printed thousands of flyers in response.

On the night in question, the competitor's agents quietly delivered pumpkins just after midnight to front porches across the area. A few hours later, the speaker's agents delivered notes saying "Hope you enjoy the pumpkins, XYZ Realty." Of course nowhere on the note did he say he actually provided those pumpkins.

My team and I tried delivering pumpkins the first year we tried farming a neighborhood, with the result that many of them broke causing quite a mess. The following year, we decided to deliver American flags on the evening before the fourth of July. Don, our friend at Gideon Promotional Products, found us large flags that were about eighteen inches across the top, and stood about two feet off the ground, at a cost of less than fifty cents each.

The key to the flag delivery was a little different than the pumpkin scenario. We selected certain neighborhoods that had many veterans. We then got a group together and delivered the flags from eight p.m. until about two a.m. We pushed the flag poles into the ground close to the street in front of each home.

When the residents of the neighborhood woke up and opened their front doors, they would see rows and rows of flags lining the street. At the bottom of each flag, we'd attach a card that said "Compliments of Loren Keim, Century 21 Keim Realtors."

Of course, we received a lot of referrals from the neighborhood, and even some 'Thank You' cards and the occasional cake from some very appreciative veterans. The sad part is that every year we delivered flags, we also received at least two or three calls from people who threatened us with lawsuits for trespassing or simply ranted at us for a half hour about putting the 'distasteful' symbol of our country in their yard,

Self Motivation and Successful Real Estate Salespeople

Earlier I wrote about failure in real estate. One of the great attractions to the industry, however, is the limitless potential for income. Remember that agent I wrote about earlier who had been living above the stalls in a barn, and progressed in her career to earning more than a million dollars a year? There are many thousands of incredible success stories across the country every single year, regardless of market conditions.

Life Lesson: Plan for your success and your more likely to achieve it.

In the late 1980's, Nancy came to work with us as a commercial land development associate in our Allentown office. Using microfiche records, she tracked down the owners of desirable vacant land parcels, determined at what price point they'd be willing to sell, and found investors and builders to purchase the properties for development.

Land development is a slow and sometimes painful process. For the first eighteen months of her career, she didn't make a dime. Her first commission check, however, nearly twenty years ago was nearly seventeen thousand dollars. Her second check was over seventy thousand. She retired from the industry after five additional years.

Our top agent in the early 1990's was a young woman who was mostly deaf. She was the sole provider for her two very young children after her husband left, taking half of the belongings. Reading the lips of her clients in order to write offers, she became very successful partly because she needed to find a way to provide for her family despite her disability.

Another agent, retired from our company, lives only a few hundred feet from the ocean in Flagler Beach, Florida. I'm jealous every time I visit.

In the early 2000's, a new associate with our firm expressed to me that he had to earn a six figure income, and he had to do it quickly. He had four children, a wife, and a mortgage to support. I explained that a lot of business exists for those willing to go out and find it. Roughly eight to ten percent of the population lists their home for sale in any given year, and several of our agents, in the past, had simply picked up the phone and called friends, relatives and random people until they found one that was thinking of selling theirs.

An agent listening in from the next room confronted me to say that realtors may no longer call at random to find possible buyers and sellers. When I give presentations at conventions, I always hear the same theme from a line of realtors who very nicely explain to me that calling potential clients is illegal because of do-not-call laws. That's not actually true. First, not everyone is signed up for the do-not-call list and secondly, there are reasons to call that do not directly involve sales.

Don't focus on what you can't do or you'll never accomplish anything. Focus on your goals and your desired outcomes, and find a path to those outcomes. Sometimes you'll have to think outside the box.

Bob, our new associate, found a list of owners of multi-unit investment properties. Sitting at his desk for a few hours a day, he called each of these investors with a simple question. "I'm calling because I noticed that you own investment properties. I own several in the area as well, and I'm a realtor specializing in real estate investment. Are you planning to add to your portfolio by purchasing more properties or planning to liquidate your properties to take advantage of the upswing in the market?"

Investors seldom stop buying and selling. Within a few weeks, Bob was producing at the same level as our top associates, proving again that anyone can be successful if they put effort and creativity into their business.

Setting Yourself Apart

One of the critical methods of developing in your career beyond your competition is to find a way to set yourself apart from that competition. Setting yourself apart might be done by providing your customers with something of value, or it might be done by specializing or it might be done by doing something outrageous.

My team and I continually tested methods of attracting attention and setting ourselves apart. We provided value to potential clients by offering free reports and free information. We specialized in specific types of properties, and we did a lot that may have been considered a bit outrageous.

Tom Cooke, a Re/Max agent who worked as a team with his wife Sally in Toronto showed me a method that he or one of the other agents he was associated with used to set themselves apart. We immediately copied the idea and have been using it on and off for years. We call it the needle-in-a-haystack box.

First, we filled a small box with hay, which is relatively easy to find in Pennsylvania. Next we purchased a package of large plastic needles that are sold at Walmart, Target and other fine retailers. Punching a hole in our team business card, we would tie the needle to our card with a piece of yarn and bury the needle in the… you guessed it, hay, placing our card on top. Last, we would close and seal the box, writing across the top "Finding a Great Real Estate Team is like finding a Needle in a Hay Stack". This was corny, perhaps, but effective.

Another of our more creative messages was our crumpled letter campaign which involved visually showing the property owner that we understand marketing and how to make ourselves stand out, which means we'll be more likely to make their home stand out.

We would print across the top of the letter "For your convenience, we have pre-crumpled this letter." Remember that the headline is what entices the prospect to actually read your message. In the letter itself, we would include language explaining why our service and marketing is a little different than the typical agent in the marketplace.

Before mailing, our team would take each letter and crumple it into a ball. Once crumpled, we'd flatten the letter again, and fold it so that the headline was immediately visible when the prospect opened the envelope.

Without giving away all my team secrets, I'll reveal one other creative marketing message. Our competitors typically sent out postcards to neighborhoods where they had recently sold a home. The postcard face would read "Just Sold" which meant everyone's cards looked virtually the same. Our goal, of course, is to entice everyone to read our message, so our postcards to the neighborhood said "Last night, your neighbor, John Smith, got exactly what he deserved… and you could be next." Of course, we were talking about a great price for his home, and virtually everyone read the card.

Remember that creativity sells like nothing else!

I'll Buy Your Home

When I put together marketing plans and creative ads, there is one thing I try never to do, and that is to mislead consumers. Realtors have a code of ethics and are forbidden from deceiving or misleading their clients at the risk of losing their license. Of course, as in any field, there are those individuals that might push the envelope of what is true or not true. Some in the field of real estate make claims so outrageous that I'm continually surprised that people actually fall for them, but sadly, as the Simon and Garfunkel song *The Boxer* says, "A man hears what he wants to hear and disregards the rest." After all, if we didn't fall for outrageous ads, companies that promise we'll lose fifteen pounds in three days would all cease to exist.

One of the most recent marketing schemes to plague us has been a plethora of realtors advertising that they will buy the client's house if it doesn't sell during the term of the listing. Appointment after appointment, home owners ask me if I'll buy their property if it doesn't sell. My response is that I'd be happy to buy it under the same conditions as my competitors, but that's seldom in the best interest of the home owner.

Of course, realtors can't buy their listings at anything close to market value. The reality is that if a realtor actually buys a home that will sell for two hundred thousand dollars, that realtor will also have to pay the closing costs which might be ten thousand or more, cover the carrying costs for mortgage, taxes and insurance for the six months the realtor has to hold onto the property, adding another twelve thousand to the cost, and pay out another ten thousand in closing costs when the realtor re-sells the property. How can a realtor purchase the home for market value and eat the thirty to forty thousand dollar loss? They can't. They would be bankrupt within weeks.

This type of advertisement was created by real estate trainers as a method for realtors to get in the door to meet with home sellers, not to actually purchase homes. We consider these to be "teaser" ads. Sadly, we all want to believe that there's a magic bullet out there that will solve all our problems, and this ad sounds really good.

The way most realtors, who use this ad, get around actually buying a home is to create a series of restrictions that significantly limit the program. For example, restrictions may include that the home seller has to pay for the home to be appraised and then set the listing price at or very close to the appraised price for a period of time and then possibly reduce it every so many days until the home's price is below market value.   The seller may be required to pay for a home inspection and a professional home stager at their cost and complete those repairs and updates before the clock starts ticking on the buyout.

Generally, the home owner also must purchase another home from the same listing agent, which eliminates any home sellers that are moving out of the area.   At this point, the home owner might say "I'm not willing to pay thousands of dollars for an appraisal, inspections, and upgrades in order to qualify for the buyout and then set my home's list price at whatever the appraiser says!"

"That's not a problem," the agent might respond. "I can still provide the best marketing program in the area with no cost upfront. I simply can't offer, however, to spend a few hundred thousand dollars to buy your home if you can't commit to spending a few thousand to make the home more saleable."

Sadly, this works. Home owners already have the agent in the room and want their home on the market. If all these restrictions fail to persuade the owner that the buyout program isn't for them, then the agent might explain that the buyout price is not the retail price at which the property is listed, but rather a wholesale price at some predetermined discount.

Does this mean that no realtor ever buys a house from a consumer? No, there are rare occasions that it happens, but honestly, if you're willing to have your home appraised, fix it up, repair anything on an inspection report and then sell it at a discounted wholesale price, *I'll* buy it.

The Human Accident Magnet

In the opening pages of this book, I mentioned an online article, written by William Bader, calling me the 'human accident magnet'. No book of my stories would be complete without at least mentioning a few of my more memorable minor traffic incidents.

Somehow, from the late 1980's into the early 1990's, I managed to become involved in somewhere north of twenty accidents. In my defense, only one of these accidents was declared as my fault. For a while, I thought I had a target painted on the side of my car. I was even t-boned by a police officer running a stop sign. After the first few, I stopped reporting them to the insurance company for fear that my insurance would be canceled and I'd be unable to replace it.

William wrote the article after speaking with a friend of his, Chris Bracy, who was in my car during one of the many near-misses that were typical of that period of my life. In this particular case, I was cruising along Route 22 in Pennsylvania, passing a major onramp from Airport Road. A driver, who was apparently planning to merge onto the highway in front of me, decided at the last minute to slam on the breaks while still on the onramp. The driver behind him, on the same ramp, was probably looking behind, planning to merge as well. Driver number two slammed into driver number one pushing him onto the highway in front of me.

I spun my steering wheel to the left, attempting to avoid the out-of-control car by shifting into the passing lane, where I cut off another car. The tractor trailer behind me must have spun his steering wheel right and jackknifed off the highway, onto the onramp. My car was untouched.

Rhonda Byrne, in her best-selling book, *The Secret*, outlined a very old concept known as the law of attraction, which, in my very limited interpretation, states that although we don't always get what we want in life, we generally get what we think about most or what we expect, whether positive or negative. If we desperately want to get out of debt and yet worry about having too much debt, we somehow seem to attract more debt. If we concentrate on not having one more car accident, we're generating some sort of negative pulse that causes us to either drive poorly, creating an accident, or be drawn to a place where an accident will likely occur.

The day after returning from his honeymoon, our mortgage guru, Bob Wilfinger, totaled his car on his way home from work when he hit a deer on Route 33 near the Poconos. The next day, he hit another deer on the same highway in the car he borrowed from his wife, totaling that as well. Try explaining two accidents on the same road in under twenty-four hours to an insurance company. Another mortgage broker, Mike O, had a total of three accidents, just outside my office, on the same road in less than two years.

Did actress Natalie Wood's fear of water somehow lead to her drowning? I don't know, and I'm not so sure about the law of attraction. There are men all over the country thinking about Jessica Alba every day, and, as far as I know, she's not showing up on their doorsteps. However, life holds many strange coincidences, and perhaps Rhonda Byrne's answer is as correct as any other.

For several years, I spent a few days each month in Saint Charles, Missouri, just west of Saint Louis. Although I occasionally flew, I often made the nine hundred mile trip by car. On one such occasion, the highway patrol diverted traffic off I-70, not far from Zanesville, Ohio, due to flooding. By the time we were halfway through the detour, all roads out of town were closed by flooding. Shelters were set up and it was the first time I remember seeing a natural disaster first-hand.

A few months later, along the same route, my wife lost control of our car and we hydroplaned into a concrete median at close to sixty miles per hour in western Pennsylvania. We were exceedingly lucky to have survived. In heavy rain, the highway drainage had backed up, flooding the road. Our car lifted off the pavement and our momentum carried us forward into the barrier. Apparently it's a really bad idea to use cruise control in the rain because tires not touching the ground actually accelerate and can cause the car to take off like a rocket.

A few months after that, I was due back in Saint Charles and planned to take my two young daughters. There was a significant ice storm crossing the path I'd have to traverse, and based on my past bad experiences, I decided not to drive. I had also recently had a bad experience on a plane to the west coast and opted for what I thought was the safest mode of transportation – an Amtrak train.

Heavy traffic made us late to the parking garage at the train station in Philadelphia. Worried about missing the train, I grabbed Bridgett and Caitlin's hands and hurried them through the parking garage. Young kids love very small plastic toys, and Bridgett was dragging a plastic bag full of her favorite ones to entertain herself during the trip. In the middle of the garage, the bag tore sending toys scattering across the parking garage floor, stopping traffic and rolling under cars. Angry and frustrated, I turned to my daughter, who was six or seven at the time, and told her that we would have to leave her favorite toys behind because we wouldn't make the train and we were holding up traffic in the garage. It was her own fault, I growled, for dragging a plastic bag.

She looked up at me, tears streaming from her eyes, and said she understood. That pained expression will haunt me for the rest of my life. Of course, we spent the next ten minutes crawling under cars and retrieving all the little toys. Ultimately, the train was nearly two hours late, so we didn't miss it.

En route to Saint Louise, by way of Chicago, using the world's safest mode of transportation, we derailed somewhere in Indiana and were taken off the train, in a blinding snow-storm, by school bus and put in a school cafeteria for shelter. There was only one injury on the train, we were informed. Amtrak was supposed to send me free tickets for another trip, but I never received them.

> *Life Lesson: Your children learn by watching you. Be the best parent you can be.*

A few years later, my wife and children flew to Orlando to meet me at a relocation conference hosted by Cendant Mobility. I was in Orlando early for the conference, when Cendant notified all participants that they were cancelling the event due to an incoming hurricane. Those, who had already arrived, left in a hurry, but my family was already en route to Florida. We spent the next day at the beautiful Marriot Sabal Palms, with mattresses taped to the large windows, as the hurricane flattened everything in its path. Ah, quality family time!

These types of stories are why William referred to me as the 'human accident magnet.' Happily, and I'm knocking on wood as I write this, the phase seems to have passed and I no longer appear to be in the middle of any accident within a fifty mile radius.

On the other hand, a few years ago, Bridgett and Caitlin were riding the *Tower of Terror* at Disneyworld's Hollywood Studios when the ride stuck, trapping them at the top for nearly two hours. Disneyworld is truly one of the greatest places on earth, and I was shocked that the ride had any issues like this. When they were finally brought down from the top, they were given complimentary fast passes to *Rock 'n' Roller Coaster*. Sadly, ten minutes after their release from *Tower of Terror*, they found themselves stuck in the middle of the *Rock 'n' Roller Coaster* ride. Maybe this accident magnet stuff is an inherited trait.

Relay for Life

At a twenty-four hour cancer walk, known as the 'Relay for Life', Michelle Miller and I were discussing Bridgett and Caitlin's unusual experience on the two separate ride failures at Disneyworld, as we trudged back to our cars to pick up more supplies for the long night ahead. Michelle joked that perhaps my daughter's were sending out some sort of electric charge that shut down the ride.

With the words barely out of her mouth, the light pole above us in the parking lot blinked out, leaving us in the dark.

"Now you're affecting electric devices," she laughed.

On the way back into the event, two more light poles blinked out as we passed beneath. Obviously, this is a strange coincidence, but perhaps Rhonda Byrne would say that the law of attraction led us toward the light poles that were most likely to go dark.

We returned to our team's area, where my wife was heating up Dinty Moore Beef Stew to help take the chill out of the cold evening. As we unpacked, I was approached by a politician and her entourage.

"Mr. Keim," she said with her hand outstretched. "It's good to see you. I hope you are supportive of our 'Stop Property Taxes Now' legislation."

I had understood that the legislation she was referring to was designed to replace school district property taxes with income taxes.

One of the challenges with charging residents high property taxes is that these taxes truly hurt those who are on fixed incomes but own houses. Post retirement, many seniors have difficulty paying these taxes, but the alternative to paying the taxes is that seniors are forced to move out of their family home.

Using an income tax to pay for schools, however, puts a burden on renters to begin paying a tax that they don't currently pay under the property tax system. Many of these tenants may be financially strapped as well. Stopping property taxes is really just shifting the burden from one group to another in order to make some politicians look good to their constituents. Another problem with the income tax, if it's collected by the state, is that the state would then have much more direct control over school districts in our area, which are currently regulated locally. If the state government is to collect the money, who is to say if a disproportionate share is suddenly sent to Philadelphia and drained from the suburban districts?

As with many issues I discuss, I don't have the solution to the problem, but I know that a quick fix to make politicians look like they're doing something positive is not the answer. I was also a little offended that someone was trying to hijack a cancer fundraiser for political gain. I replied, "I'm honestly not sure I support that platform."

She was taken aback. "So you'd rather throw our seniors out into the streets, forcing them to eat dog food?" She replied, raising her voice and attracting a crowd.

I became angry, and remembering that this particular politician had been in trouble some time ago for a DUI offense, I replied "No, I'm just sick and tired of you politician's licking your finger, sticking it in the wind to determine which way it's blowing, swallowing a few more shots, and then passing laws that affect the rest of us."

You could have heard a pin drop. I don't think I'd ever make it as a politician.

There are days when I feel that my life is a non-stop roller coaster ride with a steady stream of challenges, issues, frustration and situations that have no clear answers. Despite that, I wouldn't trade it for anything!

Afterword

Thanks to everyone who contributed to both these stories and to my life. I have been blessed in so many ways by simply knowing you, and I truly hope that I have not seriously offended any of you with the way I look at life. Some of my friends and family are very conservative and many are quite liberal in their view of the world. I have friends on one side that believe George Bush is a reincarnation of Satan and others who believe Obama is the anti-Christ. My essays are not written to offend, but rather to show another perspective that I hope each will consider.

At one point during the process of writing this book, I removed many of the political references, fearing that my words would be used against my family, and they are more precious to me than anything. Ultimately, I included them because I honestly believe we need to stop being afraid of what we say openly. I'm hopeful that someday, as a society, we can all have a dialogue about the larger issues without name calling, political spin and abject hatred.

And for those of you currently preparing hate-mail, please acknowledge that I do not want to destroy the environment, put grandmothers in the street, eliminate welfare, throw people off unemployment, hurt small children or kick puppies. We need to be good stewards of this planet we call home and of our fellow man. We need to be environmentally conscious and socially conscious, and we need to provide a safety net for those who need it, but I also believe that the reason America became the world's greatest superpower had everything to do with our individual freedom to succeed or fail and try again. Our spirit makes this country what it is, and yet our freedom is being eroded in lieu of being cared for, cradle to grave.

Certainly, some of you who know me well will wonder why I didn't include some of my more notable stories that have been passed on from group to group. I tried to limit the essays in this book to stories that could not and would not injure anyone. Some of our most painful experiences, sadly, would not only dredge up very bad memories, but may also open the individuals involved to further problems and perhaps alienate those close to me.

Some of our most humorous stories could significantly embarrass friends, family, clients, co-workers and, of course, elected officials, so I limited those as well.

Live your life to the fullest. Remember your responsibilities. And remember to stop and look around once in a while. Remember those words of Ferris Bueller, "Life moves pretty fast. If you don't stop and look around once in a while, you could miss it." Cue the music.

Loren Keim, Valentine's Day 2010.

More to come...

Interested in submitting a story to us for an upcoming book? You can submit it online at **www.backseatlifelessons.com**

Other Books by Loren Keim
Order online at www.RealEstatesNextLevel.com

How to Sell Your Home in Any Market

People sell homes every year in every market throughout the country. However in a slow real estate market, an owner must compete with other homes for fewer buyers in the marketplace. And even when the market is hot, there are still always homes that just don't sell.

The primary reasons why houses don't sell include poor staging, improper pricing, incorrect marketing, functional obsolescence and location challenges (or that people just aren't buying in the area!)

This easy-to-read, well-organized book explains how to fix your house and your sales technique to sell your home faster and for top dollar.

The Fundamentals of Listing and Selling Commercial Real Estate

A complete foundation for a career in the Commercial Real Estate Industry, the text contains a comprehensive study of property and investment analysis, mortgages and leases, as well as practice techniques such as prospecting, presentations, and negotiating.

Real Estate Prospecting: The Ultimate Resource Guide

The Ultimate Prospecting Resource: "Prospecting is a process, not an event". Filled with scripts, dialogues, sample letters, sample postcards and complete prospecting attack plans, this book is certain to help any real estate career blossom.

Short Sales: Step by Step

Loren Keim, introduces a Step by Step process for negotiating a Short Sale. Whether you are a home owner who owes more than the home can be sold for in today's market, or you're a Realtor advising clients about the process, this book is the tool you should have.

End Notes

[i] Quinn, James. <u>Quick Start to the Quinn and Rose Show</u> , 2009.
<<u>http://warroom.com</u>>.

[ii] "The Year in Review", *Las Vegas Review Journal,* 27 Dec 2009, p 3B.
"Natalie Dylan Auctions Off Virginity", *Daily Telegraph,* 12 Jan 2009,

[iii] Steven D. Levitt and Stephen J. Dubner , *SuperFreakonomics: Global Cooling, Patriotic Prostitutes, and Why Suicide Bombers Should Buy Life Insurance,* (New York: William Morrow, 2009) p 3.

[iv] Chris Carter, "Does DHS Think ACORN's Home Defenders are Left Wing Extremists?", *The Canada Free Press,* 23 May 2009.

[v] Michelle Malkin, "The Truth About ACORN's Foreclosure Poster Child", *Michelle Malkin,* 23 – Feb – 2009.
<u>http://michellemalkin.com/2009/02/23/document-drop-the-truth-about-acorns-foreclosure-poster-child/</u>

[vi] Debbie Garlicki, "City Firefighter's Girlfriend Recalls Him Shot in the Face", *The Morning Call,* 8 November 1995, sec. B, p B08.

[vii] Steven Holmes, "Fannie Mae Eases Credit To Aid Mortgage Lending", *The New York Times,* 30 Sept 1999, Sec C, p 2.

[viii] "Countrywide CEO Mozilo Announces $100 Billion, Five-Year Commitment to Low Income and Minority Home Buyers", *CSR Wire,* 5-14-2001.

[ix] "Bush Talked but No One Listened", *The Times Union,* 8 Feb 2009, sec b, p 4.

[x] Walter Williams, "Behold Congress, Deceit of Government", *Columbia Daily Tribune,* 12 Apr 2009.

[xi] Bob Unruh, "Athiests Attack Mother Teresa", *Worldnet Daily,* 02-01-10.
<u>http://www.wnd.com/index.php?pageId=122843</u>

[xii] Kraybill, Donald B.; Steven M. Nolt, David L. Weaver-Zercher (2007-09-17). <u>"Amish Grace and the Rest of Us"</u>. *Christianity Today.*
<u>http://www.christianitytoday.com/ct/2007/septemberweb-only/138-13.0.html</u>.

[xiii] Letter from Thomas Jefferson to M. L'Hommande, 1787.

[xiv] John Galt, *Dreams Come Due: Government and Economics as if Freedom Mattered,* (New York: Simon & Schuster, 1986), p 312.

[xv] JJ Blonien, "Arrest 'Silent Three' of Runaway Spending, *Wisconsin State Journal*, 30 Jan 2005, sec b, p b2.

[xvi] MC Moewe, "New Home Impact Fees Reduced", *Daytona Beach News Journal,* 11 Apr 2008, sec c, p 2c.

[xvii] Jim Gordon, "Coincidences Boggle the Mind", *Post Tribune*, 7 Feb 2006. Sec A P A3.

[xviii] Jennifer Harper, "Nation Inside the Beltway", *Washington Times,* 17 Dec 2009, sec a, p a10.

[xix] Christopher Monckton, "Scare Watch – Global Cooling is really Global Warming", *Science and Public Policy Institute*, January 2009.

[xx] Andrew C. Revkin, *New York Times,* Nov 20, 2009. Environment Section.

[xxi] "MacMillan to Seek Signs of New Ice Age; His Expedition Equipped for Polar Radio." *New York Times*, May 28, 1923.

"MACMILLAN REPORTS SIGNS OF NEW ICE AGE: Explorer Brings Word of Unusual Movements of Greenland Glaciers -- Coal Deposits Show Polar Climate Was Once Tropical." *New York Times,* September 28, 1924.

[xxii] Glenn Beck, "Glenn Beck's Common Sense", (New York: Threshold Editions) June, 2009, p. 24.

Made in the USA
Lexington, KY
04 September 2010